T0245260

"*Tas's* The Consumer Behaviour Book *brilliar* of Behavioural Economics to reveal insigh truly understanding consumers (or 'people,' ~~..~~ .... ~~..~~ .. .. (them). By challenging outdated models and advocating for a shift in thinking, Tas offers not only a clearer understanding of consumer behaviour, but also a practical framework to harness this knowledge effectively. Engaging, funny at times and meticulously researched, this book is an essential read for anyone looking to elevate their marketing strategies and truly connect with their customers."

JOHN QUINN
Head of Insight, Phoenix Group (Standard Life)

"*Behavioural Economics might not sound like a lot of fun – but* The Consumer Behaviour Book *is an easy read, delivering bite-sized chunks of wisdom interspersed with jokes and real-world examples. It should be essential reading for anyone seeking to better understand family, friends, colleagues or potential customers. Tas's book provides a practical framework to explore how we think – and how to influence human behaviour. He exposes the vagaries of human decision-making, demonstrating that (in most cases) emotion and instinct trump rationality and logic."*

ANDY BURRELL
Head of Portfolio Marketing, Nokia Cloud and Network Services

"*The most successful companies are the ones that understand their customers better than their competitors do. Tas's book will give you an unfair advantage in that regard."*

DOUGLAS BURDETT
Host of The Marketing Book Podcast

Published by
LID Publishing
An imprint of LID Business Media Ltd.
LABS House, 15-19 Bloomsbury Way,
London, WC1A 2TH, UK

info@lidpublishing.com
www.lidpublishing.com

A member of:

businesspublishersroundtable.com

All rights reserved. Without limiting the rights under copyright reserved,
no part of this publication may be reproduced, stored or introduced into
a retrieval system, or transmitted, in any form or by any means (electronic,
mechanical, photocopying, recording or otherwise) without the prior written
permission of both the copyright owners and the publisher of this book.

© Anthony Tasgal, 2024
© LID Business Media Limited, 2024

Printed and bound in Great Britain by Halstan Ltd

ISBN: 978-1-915951-20-5
ISBN: 978-1-915951-21-2 (ebook)

Cover and page design: Caroline Li

THE CONSUMER BEHAVIOUR BOOK

EXPLORING THE REASONS WHY EMOTIONS ARE SO IMPORTANT IN DECISION-MAKING

ANTHONY TASGAL

MADRID | MEXICO CITY | LONDON
BUENOS AIRES | BOGOTA | SHANGHAI

FOR OTHER TITLES IN THE SERIES ...

CONCISE ADVICE LAB

SMALL BOOKS: BIG IDEAS

CLEVER CONTENT, DYNAMIC IDEAS, PRACTICAL
SOLUTIONS AND ENGAGING VISUALS –
A CATALYST TO INSPIRE NEW WAYS OF THINKING
AND PROBLEM-SOLVING IN A COMPLEX WORLD

www.lidpublishing.com/product-category/concise-advice-series

To the memory of Daniel Kahneman (1934-2024):
wise, humble and leaving a towering legacy.

CONTENTS

PART 3: CONCLUSIONS

INTRODUCTION:
WHY DO WE NEED
A THEORY?

When interviewed about books I've written, people often ask, "How do you start writing or how do you decide what to write about?"

One bit of advice I occasionally give is to start with an issue or situation that vexes or irritates you, and discover something that you can respond to or modify.

So, in this case, something that has *really* gotten under my skin over a long period of my work life (and many people I work with professionally will be able to confirm this of me – if not for themselves) is the fact that many people who work in the business of influencing consumer behaviour through communication do not have a theory of what influence or persuasion might be, how and when it works, or how and when it doesn't.

I often asked myself why – for people immersed in the business of affecting people's choices – there seemed to be no theory or corpus of evidence or series of principles that those in the influence business would subscribe to, consciously or unconsciously, in terms of how they expected people to make those decisions.

When we see people (or even ourselves) clearly making choices that seem less than optimal or even irrational – like poor financial decisions or buying that chocolate bar when we are meant to be eating healthily – we need a theory that acknowledges rather than brushes aside the reality of consumer behaviour.

ANECDOTAGE – PART I

Although it was a slow process, the gestation of my vexation evolved from seeds planted when I was an account planner in London ad agencies back in the days of … well, that's not important.

My role was to look at the client's brand, understand its complexities, delve deep into the psyche of the target consumer and find ways of building a bridge between the two (this is pretty much the definition of 'strategy').

From there it was on to agreeing to this with the client, then formulating a creative brief to render unto the Creatives, acting as midwife to the ideas that emerged and then being part of the support team. That became the crunch point for an absence of a theory of how exactly we expected to modify behaviour (or even attitudes).

CHRONIC THEORY-AVERSION IN COMMUNICATIONS

It's a bit of a sad truth among certain practitioners of advertising that it is one of the disciplines that seems unable to learn from its past. Not just in the narrative sense of accepting errors, learning from them and achieving redemption; but more in the way that it seems chronically reluctant to embrace anything before the previous week as possibly having any intrinsic merit for the present or future.

Part of the cause is that the communications world has become more and more institutionally (or serendipitously) ageist – which is a whole topic in itself. This is mostly manifested in the *shiny shiny* attraction of the last channel – social media generally, then X (formerly known as Twitter), Instagram and TikTok – and the belief that the answer to every client, every brand, every comms problem is social media, perhaps with an added soupçon of 'influencers.' The comms world is constantly having to justify its need for 'strategy,' something that is not merely a knee-jerk reaction based on execution or medium.

But more relevant to my case here is the fact that the industry seems reluctant to learn from the enormous body of casework that it has already created, an obliviousness that will be deeply regretted.

(One of the ways, incidentally, in which advertising can learn from the law).

Creatives may learn about the likes of Bill Bernbach, David Ogilvy or George Lois when they try to hone their craft (I know this from lecturing on various ad courses for undergraduates), but they are in a minority across the industry when looking at the history of advertising (or comms) theory.

Many times I sat in meetings with my ad agency colleagues and a client or several, and arguments would erupt on the basis of an absence of shared theory. Sometimes this would be manifested in ways that now (and even then) seemed sit-com friendly: One that lingers is from a meeting with a client I worked with on a long-term basis, several geological eras ago. When we presented a variety of campaign ideas, one of which included a well-known TV personality, we waited patiently for the senior client (aka owner) to pontificate and announce whether white smoke would be issued.

We were all less shocked than we should have been when the client announced that the approval process entailed him showing it to his gardener, as "my gardener likes ads with famous people in them." (I suppose nowadays the gardener would be hailed as a 'Horticultural Influencer.')

This happened – at least at the general if not the specific, common or gardener level – with alarming frequency.

The argument from anecdote (or from creative folklore) needed something rooted in shared experience and authority.

At least the last five to ten years has seen the ad world (or at least a valiant vanguard of planners, agencies and some clients) embrace and absorb the learnings and insights of Behavioural Economics and provide something like a body of theory on which to base the creation and evaluation of communication.

Anything that can help create a shared body of theory and practice in the comms world surely has to be a good thing.

The impetus for this understanding was when I heard of something called 'Behavioural Economics.' I immediately thought this might be a theory that delivers something that everyone in the influence industry could usefully adopt. So, I'm not going to promise that I will deliver an oven-ready (sorry for the Brexit references, Brits) theory and body or evidence that is all-encompassing and ubiquitously relevant. But I will try and do three things.

One: uncover the default theories and principles that many people in this business passively absorb and often don't subject to any form of scrutiny before putting into practice.

Two: look at areas where work has been carried out that I think is progressive and helpful – in Behavioural Economics but also other areas.

And three: attempt to construct a coherent and constructive series of theories and ideas that we can use as first principles when we are working in the areas of persuasion and communication.

WHY WE NEED THEORIES (AND THEORY)
Why so keen on theory, you may ask.

Am I proposing a global theory of communications, akin to what scientists have been searching for – the so-called GUT (Grand Universal Theory) or TOE (Theory of Everything); the reasons for which I have not had adequate explanation from the scientific community, all-encompassing theories seem to have body-part related acronyms.

No, nothing that grand, but I do think some theoretical underpinning has got to be an improvement on Horticultural Influence Theory (ooh, quite a HIT).

Let's start by unpacking the theory of theory and begin with my usual jaunt into the world of etymology.

The word 'theory' comes from the Greek 'theorein,' which originally meant to look at or watch (we can still see it nesting coyly in the word 'theatre'). Some sources suggest it can be broken into two parts, the first part relating to 'theion,' meaning divine, so there is a sense of contemplation of something more vast and sublime.

Theory is needed to organize, compartmentalize and make sense of our world. Theories are models, not a replacement of reality but something that approximates to it, which can help us simplify and understand. As was said gnomically by Alfred Korzybski in 1931, "The map is not the territory."

Elsewhere, I have coined a new term to suggest that our brain is a 'patterntate,' designed by evolution to notice patterns and regularities to guide us and enhance our chances of Darwinian survival. Theories make life easier to navigate, because they act as shortcuts or heuristics.

TWO TRIBES
In a weird celebrity tag-team matchup, in the blue corner I give you Charlie Chan, the fictional private detective from Honolulu, and Chris Anderson, former editor of *Wired*, creator of *The Long Tail* article-then-book and head of TED.

And in the red corner, Charles Darwin, originator of the evolutionary theory of natural selection and regular choice as one of the Greatest Britons, partnered with Friedrich Hayek, probably one of the most famous British-Austrian economists.

Seconds out.

Let's start with Charlie Chan, who alleged, "Theory – like mist on glasses – can obscure facts."[1] But theory does precisely the opposite: it gathers, bonds and unites facts.

On the same team, I would also take umbrage at Chris Anderson. In a famous/infamous paper called "The end of theory: the data deluge makes the scientific theory obsolete,"[2] he proposed the notion that Big Data means that we no longer have a need for theory, and that this new glorious data era heralds to his eyes the triumph of correlation over causation. His paper makes it clear he is not just training his sights on the advertising world (which is part of my problem with his piece), but on the domain of *science*. But anyone versed in science – and beyond – will tell you that data needs hypotheses, models and theories on which to be hung; scientists need hypotheses to explore and test.

(For, more on this see my book, The Insight Book[3]*).*

So, let's try the other team, if only because arguably the safer option will generally be lining up on the side of Charles Darwin. For the great thinker argued that no man (sic) could be a good observer unless he was an active theorizer, cementing the connection between observation and theory that is also at the heart of the notion of insight. As his one-off tag partner, Friedrich Hayek put it, without theory, facts are dumb.

(This is also why – with my storytelling/presentation hat on – I insist that presentations are not the mute proclamation of facts, but need to have a theory, point of view and a model to bind them together: you could even call it a 'Golden Thread.')

"In theory, there is no difference between theory and practice, but in practice there is."

Attributed to US baseball coach and guru Yogi Berra

AN ALTERNATIVE TO THE MONOCULTURE THEORY

The second leg of my mission is to counter a prevailing, if implicit, set of ideas that I think are perniciously prevalent.

Let's untangle them and discuss why they are so detrimental to the business world and our understanding of consumer behaviour.

1. The Illusion of Control

So much of our behaviour as consumers and beyond depends on the notion of control, or as psychologists often describe it, 'agency' or 'effectance': the feeling that we have power over ourselves and our world.

There are very powerful reasons for this in purely evolutionary terms: that we have competence and mastery, that we can have an impact, make a difference.

If you are reading this and are British, the words 'take back control' will have a particular resonance. If you are in the US (or at least mildly familiar with US culture), it is also easy to see how the foundational myth that is the American Dream is very much premised on the idea that we are the masters of our own fates, that we can accomplish anything and be anyone that we want to be, if we just set our mind to it.

The feelings of free will, power and control are key to our sense of self, but without treading too far into the minefield of free will, we must appreciate that – as we shall see in Part 2 – our sense of control and mastery is vastly inflated, and we have much less of it than we like to think. Yet those in the business of communications persuasion insist on a theory that is based on the idea that as 'consumers' we have complete control over our decisions and actions, as they are subject to our full, conscious and rational dominion.

2. The Illusion of Self-Insight

Whether it's the Greek motto on the temple at Delphi *gnothi seauton* – "know thyself" or a hundred self-help guides, or the various therapies that offer pure enlightenment, we are all being encouraged to know ourselves better. But, as we shall see, this is not an easy task. Much of what makes us who we are – our temperament, drives, hopes – lies buried in the unconscious, which is not easily amenable to excavation.

3. Happiness

A key element of this concept of control is the goal of happiness. A veritable industry has grown up with new theories, principles and tips in seeking what now seems the ultimate human goal (at least for those who can afford it): human happiness. This cultish optimism was skewered memorably by Barbara Ehrenreich in *Smile or Die*,[4] where she dissects the power of the positive thinking industry in the US, prompted by her diagnosis with cancer. She starts by documenting some of the more outlandish claims based on her treatment and the sugar-coating she experienced by those who saw "prostate cancer as an opportunity ... to evolve to a higher level of humanity."

From this she investigates Rhonda Byrne's runaway bestseller *The Secret* with its emphasis on 'visualizing' and 'attracting' what you really desire, and the broader rise of coaching (sports, life). Again, the analysis focuses on the proximity to sympathetic or folk magic. But how much control do we actually have over our chances of achieving happiness?

4. Common Sense Isn't So Common

Duncan Watts's diatribe on the power of common sense is a salutary reminder that what we take as universal and obvious is anything but. His argument is that common sense is a shockingly unreliable guide to truth and yet we rely on it virtually to the exclusion of other methods of reasoning. In fact, common-sense explanations are often circular and constructed after the event, so common sense and history often conspire to generate the illusion of cause and effect where none exists.

5. The Monstrous Worship of Facts

Regular readers will be familiar with my obsession with what I call 'arithmocracy' and have touched on this in most of my writings: the fact that we have begun to worship unquestioningly at the altar of data and rationality, at the expense of emotion, context and meaning. An entire structure has been built on KPIs, metrics, OKRs (objective-key results), all of which has created an arid reductionism.

One example: factory managers at Ford Motor Co. produced the figures Henry Ford demanded whether they were right or not. When an edict came down that all inventory from one car model must be used before a new model could begin production, exasperated line managers simply dumped excess parts into a nearby river.

In *InCitations*, I referred to Oscar Wilde's memorable expression, the "monstrous worship of facts" from an 1891 essay,[5] where he was criticizing the obsession with factuality as an impediment to the act of writing:

"Facts are not merely finding a footing place in history, but they are usurping the domain of Fancy, and have invaded the kingdom of Romance. Their chilling touch is over everything. They are vulgarizing mankind."

Any new theory – or a key principle of a new theory – must accept that facts and the transmission of facts are not the foundation of a theory of behaviour change.

Finally, those of us in marketing understand this truism: that all business depends on selling or marketing to people, so that anything that helps us understand people better should improve our chances of commercial success. Let's begin the search for a more scientifically robust model.

The proper function of marketing is to turn human understanding into business advantage.

Let's end with a lovely dissection about how theories spread, eloquently expressed by JBS Haldane.[6] Theories become accepted, he teases, by going through the following stages.

i.   this is worthless nonsense;
ii. this is an interesting, but perverse, point of view;
iii. this is true, but quite unimportant;
iv. I always said so.

IF WE WANT TO UNDERSTAND WHY PEOPLE BEHAVE AS THEY DO – AND OUR JOB IS TO INFLUENCE IT – WE NEED A THEORY.

PART ONE

TOWARDS A THEORY OF BEHAVIOURAL ECONOMICS

AN UNBIASED NOTE ON BIAS

I would like to note here that I am not going to explore Behavioural Economics from this angle of 'humans are just a bundle of biases,' or as Steven Pinker put it, a collection of "fallacies, follies and faux pas." I find this approach reductive and misleading. The human race has clearly been doing something right from the first Greek thinkers and philosophy, science and democracy, through the Enlightenment and to modern science; the establishment of rational thinking has marked us out and produced some of mankind's greatest accomplishments.

So, I won't be pursuing the 'here's a list of biases to be wary of' method, or the three Is – Irrationalities, Inconsistencies and Imperfections; that is part of, but not the whole, (or most representative) part of the story.

WHY BEHAVIOURAL ECONOMICS?

I like to think of BE as the science (and art) of human choice, a guiding set of principles that help explore and explain why we make the decision that we do (and not the way we like to think). To shamelessly pilfer the words of American neuroscientist David Eagleman,[7] it is concerned with *why we don't think the way we think we think.*

To counter the Horticultural Influence Theory, I was desperate for anything that I could use as a defence, ideally something grounded in genuine academic authority. So, what attracted my attention initially was the fact that this rather ambiguous name (Behavioural Economics or BE) seemed to be a cover for some dramatic and radical work being done in the area that I was a practitioner in: namely, the influencing of consumer behaviour and decisions. The names – Kahneman and Tversky – were new to me, but when I heard about what they originally called Prospect Theory, it seemed a promising avenue to pursue in my hunt to discredit HIT.

At the very least, I knew that when a battle of subjectivities next arose, I could quote genuine, living and performing psychologists with years of experience and a battery of experiments and theory to back me up. Like any science, it was breathlessly new, evolving by the day but offering the hint of something new that I thought those toiling in the fields of marketing and advertising should be encouraged to be familiar with. And I knew that dangling the prospect of the word 'science' should be enough to fend off those relying on "I don't like the colour of her dress" subjectivities.

I also suspected BE could help with other elements of the agency-client interface (conflict). One battleground I found myself fighting on with irritating regularity (and the battle rages on) was on the linear nature of decisions, often wrapped in the jargonistic idioms du jour (one of the prevailing metaphors was "the customer journey" or "the customer funnel"). The very clear assumption in both these models is that things proceed in a very smooth, tidy and linear fashion.

This also played into another pocket of thinking, which was dominant in the 1970s but whose malign traces linger on, and often known as 'linear transportation models.' I discussed these in *The Storytelling Workbook*[8] that 'consumers' (or *people*, as I still prefer to think of them) go through a precisely defined set of stages, culminating in the client's Holy Grail of Purchase.

The most famous is still probably AIDA (which has an annoyingly operatic memorability to it too: awareness, interest, desire, action). This model – which enjoyed some popularity from the 1950s (and still rears its unattractive visage) – is a glorious example of the belief that these events have to happen in the pre-defined order. Even at the dawn of my ad career, it was clear that this was untenable: why did awareness have to be created first? Who said interest came next? Why did desire have to make do with bronze? What if action was the first goal of communication?

Might there be some theory that disproved – or at least challenged – these models?

THE MYTH OF
HOMO ECONOMICUS

One of the central tenets of BE – and what made it immediately appealing to those of us working in the influence and persuasion industries – was how it took on the default model that seemed to operate in a clandestine and yet powerful way not only with clients (of all levels) but also – as I found from lecturing – even with students and young people entering the business.

The model is generally known as Homo Economicus, as it represents a series of assumptions about human decision-making and choice, which have been the preserve of classical (or Neo-classical, if you're in *The Matrix*) economics and have been handed down and shared for generations, from government to business, and are equally prevalent in B2B and B2C universes.

Broadly speaking, these nesting and interlocking assumptions are:

1. That people are predominantly (or even maybe exclusively) rational in their behaviour. When we make decisions – be it which brand of yoghurt to buy, what paper to read, which telecoms company to use, this is a purely rational sequence of events.

2. The choices they make follow the same pattern in that they are wholly or largely rational in nature.

3. That these choices are also largely consistent from moment to moment.

4. So, for those communicating with and trying to affect people's choices or buying decisions, this implies a theory of communications that must be – again – largely based on facts and rationality, because that is what the 'consumer' wants (or thinks they want).

5. This implies a principle that only *conscious persuasion* can work to influence behaviour.

6. And finally, one of the terms used by classical economists, which never ceases to bring a smile to my jaundiced face: that we maximize utility. This precept, integral to neo-classical economics since its inception by utilitarian thinkers such as Jeremy Bentham, is that people will always seek to make the best possible decision they can to achieve personal satisfaction. Sound obvious? Common sense, yes? Don't we all, as omniscient consumers, unceasingly strive to make the best decision that is most likely to contribute to our own happiness? But think on it a minute: Are you sure? Every decision? Do you really consciously strive to optimize at every moment?

This canonical model has been surprisingly prevalent in the business world. Perhaps because many practitioners are steeped in economics; perhaps because so many large companies have accountants at their pinnacle; perhaps because it feels, well, so plausible. Perhaps because like so many theories, it just plugs a gap.

At the destructive heart of this is the economic philosophy of neoliberalism, which to many leads to a worldview based on a reduction of all social life to the logic of profit-seeking behaviour.

(Not to mention the fact that these rational behaviours are more susceptible to measurement in market research terms. So many measurements – especially measures of likely behaviour change, recall and purchase intention – assume conscious awareness of facts and are predicated on the validity of this model.)

Experts in the field have become increasingly dismissive of Homo Economicus. My favourite takedown is from a professor of human evolutionary biology, Joseph Heinrich at Harvard. In an interview with fellow evo-bio specialist David Sloan Wilson on the Evonomics website,[9] he discusses how his team tested the predictions of the HE model across a diverse range of human societies, but found no evidence that confirmed its validity.

"Nevertheless, after our paper 'In search of Homo Economicus' in 2001 in the American Economic Review, *we continued to search for him. Eventually, we did find him. He turned out to be a chimpanzee. The canonical predictions of the Homo Economicus model have proved remarkably successful in predicting chimpanzee behaviour in simple experiments. So, all theoretical work was not wasted; it was just applied to the wrong species."*

Don't let anyone tell you scientists don't have a sense of humour.

But why does this cherished narrative and 'neural fairy tale' (as Linda Feldman Barrett famously called it) of Homo Economicus refuse to die? Why do so many people I meet in the business (newcomers and stalwarts) carry this around implicitly (sometimes explicitly)?

ECONOMISTS: LOOK AWAY NOW

"Economists have predicted all nine of the last five recessions."[10]

"There can be no knowledge without emotion. We may be aware of a truth, yet until we have felt its force, it is not ours. To the cognition of the brain must be added the experience of the soul."

British novelist Arnold Bennett[11]

ANECDOTAGE PART II

Flashback to 2010.

I had been freelancing with an ad agency, helping to work with the (then) Labour government in the UK on developing an anti-bullying strategy aimed at young people. After a general election that year, the government then shifted to a coalition led by Conservative PM David Cameron, and he was one of the first government leaders to pick up on the ideas that had gained traction in the book Nudge[12] *by Richard Thaler and Cass Sunstein (first published in 2008). It had already attracted the attention of an up-and-coming politician in Chicago, called Barack Obama (Obama and Sunstein were both law professors there in the 1990s, and Obama came into Thaler's orbit in 2004 as a senate hopeful in Illinois.)*[13-15]

Soon after becoming President, Barack Obama established a unit – officially known as the Social and Behavioural Sciences Team (SBST) – to use insights from psychology, Behavioural Economics, and other decision sciences to improve federal programs and operations.

In 2010, the UK Cabinet Office took note and published a document-cum-think piece to outline the new ideas swirling around BE, under the name (acronym, actually) of MINDSPACE.[16]

This grabbed my attention, as it suggested that our government was paying attention to this body of theory that might justify what many of us in the comms world had suspected.

One paragraph challenged the orthodoxy in this way:

"More generally, there is increasing understanding across the behavioural sciences about the factors that shape and affect our behaviour, in contrast – or complement – to legal and regulatory instruments conventionally used to compel us to behave in particular ways."

But it was this sentence that really stopped me in my tracks:

"This shifts the focus of attention away from facts and information, and towards altering the context within which people act. We might call this the 'context' model of behaviour change."

Here was a government body declaring to the world that they needed to "move away from facts and information." To me this looked like an admission, one of guilt, relief and belated honesty: after all these decades where government information departments had put out ad campaigns encouraging people to change their behaviour (for example, to stop smoking, drive more slowly, eat more healthily), here they were stating (as directly as their anxious legal team would allow, I suspect) that ... maybe ... they didn't *actually* work? Or maybe they had ceased working over time?

So, to take some examples: to cut down smoking, we would have to be bombarded with a barrage of information about the evils of smoking; to eat more healthily would entail being fed a plethora of facts about the perils of a poor diet. Yet did this – and does this – affect consumer behaviour?

This chimed with much of what we had felt in the ad industry: just telling people facts and information seemed to be ineffective or at least subject to the law of diminishing returns. This was especially so if they were facts and information that people were already overfamiliar with – for instance, that smoking was bad for you, could affect your lungs and decrease your longevity.

But who doesn't know this? Years of exposure to these data and facts have become increasingly futile in cutting through, and this is what I found so shockingly illuminating. And if the UK government was going to acknowledge these (painful?) truths, so much the better for the comms industry at large.

This could be the start of a new theory of behaviour change that we could work with.

BE LESS DISMAL

In an 1849 essay on slave owning in the West Indies, Scottish essayist and philosopher Thomas Carlyle[17] attacked political economy as "... a dreary, desolate, and indeed quite abject and distressing (science); what we might call ... **the dismal science**."

Might it be possible to construct a blend of different sciences, methodologies and approaches ... a happy, joyous, fun and serendipitous science and one that would be effective in changing behaviour?

A BRAIN-SHAPED DETOUR INTO THE MIND

"I've read that the brain is the most amazing thing in the universe. But look what's telling us that."

Comedian Emo Philips.

The reason our failures to affect consume behaviour occur so often, I suggest , is that they are based on a flawed understanding of our brain.

We can't build the foundations of our theory into consumer behaviour and substantiate it without understanding how our brain works and ensuring that any theory we build works *with* the brain rather than (as Homo Economicus does) *against* it.

MAKE IT EASY ON YOURSELF

DANGEROUS
MENTAL METAPHORS

First, let's dispense with some unhelpful metaphors.

In case you haven't read *The Storytelling Workbook*, let me briefly remind you of two dangerously misleading metaphors that are often unconsciously present when we think of behaviour change and communication.

Please refrain from imagining that the brain of your audience is like a sponge, ready to soak up and retain the stream of information you are directing at them. The brain is not a sponge, porously prepared to absorb and retain. Neither is it a computer, processing and conserving everything in its memory.

(There is a wonderful cartoon by Gary Larson of a student raising his hand saying, *"Mr. Osborne, may I be excused? My brain is full."*)

So, how often have you felt yourself faced with a mind-numbing quantity of information designed to make you choose the best/right option, and yet you find yourself running away screaming and choosing the easiest one?

THE VERY MODEL
OF A BRAIN

We have to start, I feel, with the analogy of Lisa Feldman Barrett[18]: her analysis begins with the fundamental assertion that the brain is metabolically the most expensive organ in the body. So, if we stop regarding the brain as a computer or sponge with endless resources to make the perfect and optimal calculation at every moment, and instead see it as an energy-conserving organ, an entirely different picture emerges. Barrett calls this the brain's 'body budgeting.'

So, what does this say about the brain?

1. *Effortlessness* is arguably the most important guiding principle of the brain. This happens whether we are aware of it or not. To be as energy efficient as it can, the brain creates shortcuts (also known as heuristics) that minimize the amount of repetitive heavy lifting it has to do. So in many senses, the most pertinent definition of intelligence is *effortlessness*, precisely because more intelligent brains use less power. Research indicates that in intelligent people's brains, links are more efficient and better organized. It has also been said that the brain accounts for around 2% of the average person's body weight, but it consumes 20–25% of all the energy the body needs. That one scrap of data is enough to explain the brain's role and make clear why economists who wish us all to be maximizers of our utility are

failing to comprehend the effect that optimizing energy has on our brain and its choices.

2. Our brain and nervous systems pay attention to things that are biologically relevant: things without biological consequence get passed by. This is something that is not sufficiently known and/ or acted on by those in the communications world.

3. The brain is an Unrelenting Prediction Generator (UPG?), constantly emitting streams of predictions and hypotheses to test itself against the world. It simulates the consequences and then checks and corrects them against real sensory experience. One example: what Edgar Allan Poe termed 'The Imp of the Perverse': why do we sometimes find ourselves on the top of a steep building with an urge to jump? In no sense can this be seen as beneficial to us as an individual, or to our group, surely. Dean Burnett, neuroscientist, stand-up comedian and author has an explanation: that our brains are constantly running models and simulations to improve our knowledge of the world around us to enhance our chances of Darwinian success; often these hypotheticals are out on the edge precisely to test out existing boundaries and assumptions. Add to this the fact that our brains are more attuned to what is negative and threatening and that signals from these events are more likely to be memorable, and then the 'should I jump?' sensation becomes more explicable.

4. So, emotion, feeling and biological regulation all play a role in human reason: "Nature appears to have built the apparatus of rationality not just on top of the apparatus of biological regulation, but also from it and with it," as neuroscientist Antonio Damasio puts it.[19]

5. Our brain also operates, in the words of social psychologist Timothy Wilson,[20] as a form of *psychological immune system*. Just as we are endowed with a powerful physical immune system that protects us from threats to our physical wellbeing, so the brain is a form of psychological immune system whose role is to protect us from threats to our psychological wellbeing. This is why we find that our brain protects us by making us want to be liked, to be superior, and to be consistent.

TO BOLDLY THINK
A brief thought experiment.

Think of your favourite *Star Trek* iteration of Captain James Tiberius Kirk, and Vulcan's finest, Mr. Spock. (For me it's William Shatner and the late Leonard Nimoy). The creator of *Star Trek*, Gene Rodenberry, was keen on displaying (albeit in rather unsubtle terms) the rational/emotional divide, so created a race – the Vulcans – who have no emotions (or are able to fully repress them).

So here is the experiment: why would a race without emotions almost certainly fail to survive?

When I ask this in workshops, I usually get a variety of responses, the most common being that they would never reproduce, so the race would die out. Or maybe that without fear they would be prey to all sorts of predators.

But the answer that philosophers and BE advocates give is simpler: without the ability to have emotions, they would be incapable of coming to a conclusion; unable to make decisions, they would be forever stuck in a Möebius loop of infinite rational evaluation.

Because ultimately, we need our emotions to override rationality (especially in times of mental stress) and deliver us an answer that feels right.

The professor of psychology, author and henchman of Derren Brown, Richard Wiseman, told me a story about how psychologists recommend making up your mind.

Imagine you have a choice – say, whether to buy this car, dress or season ticket for Man Utd. You take a coin, and you tell yourself, "Heads I do buy this. Tails I don't." You toss the coin, examine where it falls *and then see how you feel*. If your gut feeling is, "OK, best of three," you know what you really want to do.

In Antonio Damasio's *Descartes' Error* (1994) and *The Feeling of What Happens* (1999), he tells the story of Phineas Gage.[21]

Gage became a cause célèbre in the emotions business after Damasio popularized the story of the railman who survived a tamping iron being blown through his head. Despite never actually losing consciousness, he was able to talk and walk shortly after the accident and was up working within hours; despite everything, he lived another 12 years of life.

Though he resumed work, his mood and personality changed: "Gage was no longer Gage," being described thus:

"... fitful, irreverent, indulging at times in the grossest profanity (which was obviously considered much worse back then) ... capricious and vacillating ... his mind was radically changed, so decidedly that his friends and acquaintances said he was 'no longer Gage.'"

The damage to his brain affected his emotions, leaving him unable to function not because his ability to rationalize had been affected, but because his social and moral functioning were irreparably impaired. This suggests that damage to our emotions is more critical than defects of rationality.

It is the emotions that control and guide our behaviour, as consumers and beyond.

Damasio illustrated his theory of the link between frontal lobes, emotion and decision-making. Gage became one of the most famous patients in medicine, his case being a founding example in neurology and modern behavioural sciences.

Note for those interested in the naming of scientific papers: the original scientific paper in the *Boston Medical and Surgical Journal* written in 1868 by Dr John Harlow had the graphically simple title: "Recovery from the passage of an iron rod through the head."

So, the next time you find yourself in front of a shelf or on a website, and you can feel your brain screaming in agony, your brain is telling you that your behaviour is hurting it.

TO INFLUENCE CONSUMER BEHAVIOUR, THEN, WHAT PRINCIPLES CAN WE PUT IN PLACE FROM BEHAVIOURAL ECONOMICS?

PART TWO

KEY
PRINCIPLES

PRINCIPLE 1: THINKING BEYOND RATIONALITY

"If we stopped doing everything for which we did not know the reason, or for which we cannot provide a justification, we would probably soon be dead."

Friedrich Hayek[22]

" ... (we have a) ... satisfying but illusory impression that our morals are based on reasoned and logical thought rather than cartoonesque reflexes such as yuk or ouch ..."

Cordelia Fine[23]

"Darwin ... showed us that our emotions don't entirely belong to us. And that though we might fondly imagine ourselves to be the drivers of our bodies, we are more like passengers, along for a ride."

Tiffany Watt Smith[24]

"Reason is, and ought only to be, the slave of the passions."

David Hume, *Treatise on Human Nature*[25]

"What we call rational grounds for our beliefs are often extremely irrational attempts to justify our instincts."

TH Huxley[26]

Irish humourist Jonathan Swift wrote to fellow satirist Alexander Pope that he was preparing a treatise (which would later become *Gulliver's Travels*). Swift wanted to give a fresh perspective on the comment attributed to Aristotle that man (sic) is a "rational animal":

"... [my] aim is to prove the falsity of that definition animal rationale (man is a reasoning creature) and to show it should only be rationis capax (man has the ability to reason). Upon this great foundation of misanthropy ... the whole building of my Travels is erected."

Bear this in mind when addressing or attempting to change human behaviour: we are *capable* of rationality.

THE LADDER OF RATIONALITY

It has always been mankind's overweening belief in itself and its rationality that has contributed to our sense of superiority, our position at the top of what was referred to as the Scala Naturae, a ladder with God at the top, but humans ahead of all other Creation.

The Scala Naturae (Ladder of Creation) is a special example of reductionism, later famously named "The Great Chain of Being" by Arthur Lovejoy. This will be familiar to most people from the clichéd image of the *amoeba to monkey to man* in the evolution of mankind.

The number of ads, in particular, that have borrowed this myth – and added weight to its plausibility – is legion. You remember: starting on the left you see the first 'Neanderthal Man' barely able to crawl, who turns into 'Upright Man,' who walks but still looks unmistakeably apelike, before finally evolving into 'Modern Man.' You can tell he's modern because he uses, endorses or promotes our brand.

The potency of this ideology explains why this icon of progress is still with us everywhere we go.

It was this hierarchical, deeply conservative applecart that Darwin's insights began to upset. His theory described a process that was bottom up in its direction, but that did not necessarily involve a sequence of improvements or any notion of accumulated progress.

Part of the lure of the ladder was that it reinforced the prevailing Christian worldview that man was the summit of all things living, but was subject to the mind and will of God. Nowadays the preferred model is the tree or bush, which radiates in different directions and has no sense of either progress or improvement, divine or otherwise: just blind Darwinian variation. And rationality is part of the justification for our place there.

In myth and religion too, the ladder always offers something that is divine and perfect at its summit (more accurately at its 'climax': the Greek for 'ladder'). Jacob's Ladder (as well as being a great 1990 Adrian Lyne movie, with a pre-Shyamalan shock ending) was a tale from Genesis where the patriarch sits down and dreams of a ladder reaching up to the heaven with the angels of God ascending and descending.

(Anyone recognize this in their company, brand or agency?)

Blame Plato. His metaphor of rationality and emotion pulling in different directions created a path that has been hard to escape: the notion that horses are the emotions, wayward and wilful, and reason is the charioteer trying to impose control and discipline.

But maybe reason/rationality and emotions are not destined to be eternally at loggerheads?

And even Aristotle, remember, said humans were a 'rational animal' ('logikon' in the original Greek). He wasn't underestimating our animal instincts and drives.

Darwin is a font of wisdom on this topic, and also accepted the limits of rationality (known as 'bounded rationality' and coined by economist Herbert Simon).

"Men are called creatures of reason: more appropriately, they would be creatures of habit."

Charles Darwin

So, we must acknowledge that our lives are not driven primarily by rational arguments and motives. Rationality is not the only game – or indeed the main game – in town.

A better analogy comes from a paper by Jonathan Haidt: think of, he says, the emotional dog and its rational tail. At heart we are emotional dogs who signal using our rational tails. Reasons come later; they are often used mainly for social consumption and justification.

One final thought. When I was an agency planner, working on the Peugeot account in Paris, I would make frequent trips to their Paris office, usually to help negotiate a truce between the different factions. One day I passed someone's office, and saw this:

"Le rationnel est l'alibi du désir."

Even in this Google-able era, I have still failed to find a source for this insight, but it still resonates: the rational is the alibi of desire. (Everything sounds better in French). So, let's face the naked truth: those of us engaged in the art of persuasion and influence can re-frame our jobs; we are in the business of finding alibis for desire.

(If you are someone who still has a business card, or fancy changing your social media description, I think you could do worse than describe your prime directive as 'finding alibis for desire.')

WHAT IS THE REASON FOR RATIONALITY?
"Freud not only showed how irrational we are, but how irrational rationality is."[27]

Adam Phillips

So, if reason and rationality are not at each other's throats, how should we view them?

Philip Tetlock argues that conscious reasoning is carried out largely for the purpose of persuasion rather than discovery, and this is the basis of what I like to call the M&S theory (sometimes known as the Justification Hypothesis) proposed by Hugo Mercier and Dan Sperber. In *The Enigma of Reason*[28] and elsewhere, they posit that much of the experimental evidence suggests that people quite often arrive at their beliefs and decisions with little or no attention to reasons; reasons are for social consumption, so humans are the 'justifying animal.'

So, reasons, according to Mercier and Sperber, serve two major social functions: a *justificatory* function and an *argumentative* function.

Part of their justification of the Justification Hypothesis is found in exploring the philosophical tradition, which gives me the opportunity to delve into the story of 5th century BCE Athenian philosopher, Socrates. Famous for his awkwardness (he was nicknamed the gadfly for his constant gnawing irritation), his demise is well-known: when accused of corrupting the youth of Athens, he took hemlock and committed suicide (the subject of Plato's *Apology*). He is also remembered for maxims such as, "the unexamined life is not worth living" and "all I know is that I know nothing" (it's not hard to imagine why he was considered such a pain).

But the Socratic dialectical method, known as the elenchus,[29] is a form of quasi-cooperative questioning (or maybe more like interrogation), toing and froing, to test and ideally improve a hypothesis or line of thinking. For M&S, Socrates typifies this social nature of argument: that reason exists primarily to convince others.

PICK A CARD

In 1969, British cognitive psychologist Peter Wason[30] devised a simple experiment to test out our power of logical reasoning. Subjects are shown four cards, some with a number, some with a colour. They are told each card has a number on one side, and a colour on the other.

The cards include the numbers three and eight and the colours green and blue.

The goal is to determine whether this rule has any exceptions: if one of these cards has an even number on one side, then its other side is green.

The question is which cards do you have to turn over to determine whether that is true? Fewer than half the subjects guess correctly.

The correct answer is that you must turn over only the eight card and the blue card. Here is an explanation for each of the cards:

- **The three card:** does not need to be turned over, because it is not even, so it cannot trigger the stated proposition.

- **The eight card:** even, so it must be turned over, because if the other side is not green, then the proposition is not true.

- **The green card:** many people choose this card, but it does not need to be turned over, because if the other side is odd, then the proposition is not tested, and if the other side is even, that is consistent with the proposition, but it does not prove or disprove the truth of the proposition.

- **The blue card:** does need to be turned over, because if the other side is even, then the proposition is not true.

But if we change the form (not the content) and turn it into a more social form of reasoning, different results emerge. In this case, imagine you are a bouncer in a bar and your task is to ensure no underage drinking is permitted. Here, the cards carry information about age on one side of the card and what is being drunk on the other side. Now which cards need to be turned over?

The cards include Coke, beer, 25 years old, 16 years old.

Why does this version perform better? (It's 16 and beer, by the way.)

In the first case, the test is abstract; the second is more concrete, social and relatable. This test is also a seminal example for proving the power of confirmation bias: that most subjects tend to choose cards that are capable of confirming the statement rather than disconfirming.

So, why exactly is the brain a pretty good scientist, but an even better lawyer seeking arguments and justifications? The brain seems to start with a conclusion, find a story and then only later seeks evidence to confirm it.

Which explains ...

- *Much of our behaviour is automatic and makes us feel good, and we don't forensically examine why we like that beer, read that paper or choose to vote one way or espouse that cause.*

So instead, we need to ...

- *Frame our brands and create communications that do not assume we are talking to independent scientists but lawyers looking to justify a case.*

Which brings us to ...

PRINCIPLE 2:
WE ARE MOSTLY
UNCONSCIOUS

"I do not hesitate to maintain that what we are conscious of is constructed out of what we are not conscious of."

Sir William Hamilton[31] 1865.

I've always had a lot of time for a *Time* headline[32] from 2015 for an article looking at the effect of the movie *Inside Out*, referring to scientists examining the premise of the Pixar movie. The article highlights the fact that the conscious mind tends to be seen as the president/CEO and gets all the glory and kudos; but so much actually transpires in the unconscious, which tends to get left out of the limelight.

Why do we resist this neuroscientific truth?

Simple. Because it goes against the grain that we are in control, with our conscious rational faculties keeping a tight rein (Plato's metaphor) on things, not acceding to our 'dangerous' emotions. This is more prevalent in some countries than others (evidence is hard to come by, but my experience suggests Anglo-Saxons are more reluctant to acknowledge the power of emotion).

A ONE AND A TWO

The terms System 1 and System 2 have become more familiar over the years largely to those who have read Daniel Kahneman's *Thinking Fast and Slow*.[33] Though popularized by Kahneman and Kahnemaniacs, the terms were originated by Keith Stanovich and Richard West.

The reason I start with Stanovich[34] is that before the more popular adoption of the dual system theory of cognitive processing known as System 1 and System 2, Stanovich wanted to avoid the notion that System 1 was a single unified system, so he coined the acronym TASS – The Autonomous Set of Systems.

Apologies, but couldn't resist.

Two minds in one brain, as he puts it in *The Robot's Rebellion*, describing TASS as "the parts of the brain that ignore you."

Let's take a brief look at how the two systems work so we can use them as the basis for a (sharp intake of breath) global theory of communications.

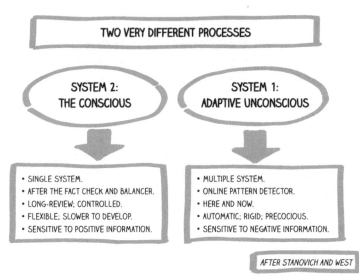

FIGURE 1

And slightly counterintuitively, let's start with 2 before 1.

System 2 is effectively the explicit, rational and analytic system usually summarized as the 'conscious.' It tends to operate after the fact as a fact-checker and balancer; it is (gently) more interested in the longer view and has a more controlled perspective.

System 1, on the other hand, is more autonomous, implicit and is composed, like the fabled Swiss Army Knife, of multiple systems or modules. What marks it out as a separate process is the fact that it is automatic, which can lead to its actions and predictions being rigid or even precocious. And of great significance is the fact that this is all happening without our conscious knowledge or participation, so System 1 is often known as the Adaptive Unconscious.

But the adjective carries a burden too: it is where evolution plies its trade silently but potently to ensure that, as individuals, we carry out evolution's prime directive that we successfully navigate our lives and pass on our genes. (This is often referred to as the modern Darwinian Synthesis, Richard Dawkins's selfish gene being just one component of that theory.)

In other words, the unconscious adapts to ensure that we survive and thrive, but – and this is crucial – much of what it does to help this adaptation goes on without our knowledge and agreement. So, evolution primes System 1 to be constantly on the watch for what can affect our lives; this means System 1 is focused entirely on the here and now.

Hence, in Thaler and Sunstein's terms, if you believe in Homo Economicus and see System 2 as the controller, you are an 'Econ': only by accepting the reality that System 1 is in charge are you truly human.

UNCONSCIOUS ELEPHANTS

In social psychologist Jonathan Haidt's *The Happiness Hypothesis*[35] (and later built on by Chip and Dan Heath in *Switch*[36]), there is an elegant and memorable metaphor for the relationship between the two systems (and that goes beyond it, too).

Haidt conjures up the memorable image of an elephant and rider.

In this metaphor, the rider is System 2 perched aloft the elephant, seemingly in control of the animal. But the potency of this analogy lies precisely in highlighting the false impression the rider has:

because whether the rider knows and admits it or not, the elephant does what it wants. Its evolutionary instincts lead it where it wants, no matter what the rider believes. So, instincts and drives such as the need for water or food, the presence of a potential enemy aggressor or a likely mate – these are what attract or repel the elephant. In evolutionary terms, the other joy of this metaphor is that we can see not only that the elephant (aka System 1) is in charge, but in fact the rider only evolved to serve the elephant.

Before we depart this delightful analogy, I'd like to examine one other element that Chip and Pin (sorry, that's just how I remember them) bring to Haidt's original concept. The third component of understanding the brain and the process of behaviour change is that of *context*.

To the picture of System 1 as the emotions and drives of the elephant, System 2 as the rational rider trying to justify to themselves that the elephant is under their command, we can add the importance of context (Chip and Pin call it the 'path'). In other words, behaviour change does not just depend on talking to the rider (System 2), or even just focusing on the elephant (System 1); the path is also a crucial component in the behaviour change mix, as it can guide the elephant/System 1.

To return to Daniel Kahneman, he calls System 1 "the secret author of our choices."

As we saw earlier, the brain is designed (as with much of evolution's work) to be as parsimonious as possible.

BATS, BEARS
AND SNAKES

MINDLESSNESS

So much of what we do is literally mindless.

There is extensive literature on the concept of mindlessness, much of it pioneered by Brian Wansink, professor of consumer behaviour and a specialist in nutrition psychology, notably on how people make food choices and the significance of portion sizes.[37]

One of the experiments is about soup bowls (soup appears with surprising frequency in food psychology literature).

In 2005, his lab published a paper based on an experiment making use of a clever apparatus containing a tube that pumped soup into the bottom of a bowl at a constant rate as the subjects were eating. The study found that those who ate from the bottomless bowl ate more soup than those whose bowls were filled manually, as the latter group was more (consciously) aware of the amount they ate.

Wansink advocated a form of 'stealth health' and believed that when fighting the fat, and trying to eat healthily, changing your eating environment is actually easier than changing your mind (the path rather than the elephant using the recent analogy) and that subtle tweaks involving plates, serving spoons, spouses, cupboards and colours can be hugely effective in changing diet.[38]

Here are some other findings that demonstrate the power of context ('path') to affect our behaviour mindlessly.

* Not leaving snackable and tempting food out on the counter where it is (to use the word psychologists favour) 'available.'

- They found that people tend to focus on the height of what they pour and not the width: we pour 12% less wine into taller glasses than if we use wider wine glasses that hold the same amount.

- Big plates mean big portions. We eat 22% less from a 25-cm plate than from a 30-cm one. And we eat significantly more when the plate colour matches the food.

- When the glass is on the table, people pour 12% less than if they were holding it in their hand.

LOVE AND UNCONSCIOUS AROUSAL

This means we can also be wrong about why we are feeling what we are feeling. This helps explain the bizarre phenomenon of Stockholm Syndrome, of hostages seemingly feeling empathy for their kidnappers; anxiety is misinterpreted as a form of liking.

Robert Epstein[39] is a research professor at the California School of Professional Psychology in San Diego and one of his main subjects – The Love Project – has been to debunk Hollywood myths of how we fall in love. In his view, love is not magical or special, but he reckoned anyone could fall in love given the right circumstances.

As he put it in an interview in 2003:

"Romantic love has failed, and dating is absurd. We need to choose someone with whom there is a basic compatibility and with whom we share some attraction – and make a conscious, serious and sustained effort to learn to love them."[40]

Clearly no fan of fairy tales, he believes that love is not, "magic, mysterious and meaningful coincidences. It's science." And he has clearly set himself in opposition to some of our longest-standing and deepest myths, claiming that he has "hacked love." (His team carried out an analysis of arranged marriages and found surprisingly high levels of love building over time within them.)

Perhaps his most controversial recommendation is that couples sign love contracts to take more control over their love lives. Not just a theory, but to put it to the test, he took the unusually practical (for a scientist) step of signing a contract that tied him to a woman he barely knew. According to the agreement, he and his new partner had to spend the following four months learning to fall in love with each other.

(Spoiler alert: this love story did not have a happy ending. His partner, a Venezuelan socialite – and former Miss Venezuela – ended the experiment, declaring, "I can't do it, I can't do it.")

A BRIDGE TOO FAR

In 1974, two Canadian psychologists, Donald Dutton and Arthur Aron, conducted an experiment[41] on the spectacular Capilano Suspension Bridge in British Columbia, Canada, which rises some 230 feet (70 metres) above the river. (Vertigo sufferers can skip the next three paragraphs.)

A female research assistant was asked to approach lone male tourists at the entrance to the bridge. She was then instructed to invite the men to walk to the middle of the dauntingly high bridge and write an imaginative story in response to a drawing. Afterwards, the researcher gave each participant a telephone number to call if he wanted to find out the results of the research project.

Dutton and Aron then repeated their experiment but this time on a different, nearby bridge. This one was quite sturdy and was only ten feet (three metres) above the river. This time the tourists would write their stories in the middle of a bridge that posed no threat and therefore aroused no fear.

The results showed that 65% of the men on the first bridge rang the telephone number provided and asked for a date, while only 30% of those on land did. The researchers concluded that this was due to a 'misattribution of arousal'. The men on the scary bridge felt an adrenalin surge and a rush of blood to the head, both physical responses associated with fear – but they had mistaken vertigo for lust.

Another study by Gregory White of the University of Maryland also examined misattribution of emotion. In his experiment, a group of men were told to run in place to elevate their heart rate before being asked to rate the attractiveness of a woman. The control group ran for only a few seconds. The result was the same: the rush of adrenalin (this time prompted by physical exercise) was mistaken for sexual ardour.

So, in the heat of the moment, we often make rash, hurried and irrational decisions, and we can be wrong about why we are feeling what we are feeling.

What this phenomenon also demonstrates is that our arrow of causality is often sadly misdirected. We know that when we find someone attractive, our hearts beat faster. But what these arousal experiments also prove is that the converse can be true: when our hearts beat faster, we are more likely to find someone seductive. In other words, much of what we feel is under our control is not and many of the signals we receive are false.

"Each of us is a single narrative which is constructed continually, unconsciously, by, through and in us."

Oliver Sacks[42]

CREEPY BUT TRUE

"There's someone inside my head and it's not me."

Pink Floyd[43]

What makes us uncomfortable about this is that a number of upsetting implications fall out from this picture.

* There are forces inside you that are controlling your brain
* You are not [consciously) aware of them
* These forces might not be acting in your best interests
* That what you think of as your 'self'/your 'I' doesn't actually control your brain
* Because your brain is built to serve evolution and your genes not you.

SYSTEM 1 RULES

Let's go back and take another look at our sense of control.

One of my favourite quotations on the power that System 1 exerts over us comes from social psychologist Timothy Wilson in his book *Strangers to Ourselves*.[44]

"Many of people's chronic dispositions, traits and temperaments are part of the adaptive unconscious, to which they have no direct access."

Try this little maths question out to see how much (or little) conscious control you have, especially when under pressure.[45]

A bat and a ball cost $1.10 in total. The bat costs $1 more than the ball. How much does the ball cost?

If you're like 90% of people (and 50% of maths students) you will say 10c.

Devised by Yale Professor Shane Frederick as part of a CRT (Cognitive Reflection Test) in 2005 and popularized (again) in *Thinking Fast and Slow*,[46] it is a clear demonstration that our gut instinct, our instinctive reaction (under the control of System 1) can often make quick and unreflective – and thus faulty – decisions. It is only when System 2 is activated that recognition occurs that 10 cents is not the correct answer.

(Check the endnotes for the correct answer. And trust me – that is the correct answer.)

So far so obvious: System 1 is the secret author of our choices and decisions but can lead us astray.

Now let me show you the same information, but in a different format (Figure 2).

A bat and a ball cost $1.10 in total.
The bat costs $1 more than the ball.
How much does the ball cost?

FIGURE 2

If I tell you now that significantly more people get the answer right when presented with the information here, that may seem strange. But the answer is quite revealing and allows me to devise a tentative global theory of communication off the back of it.

Pause for breath.

So, why is this version more likely to achieve a correct answer? It seems to be because although the *facts* are the same, the *presentation* is subtly but crucially different.

1. It is deliberately in a smaller font than version one
2. It is in italics
3. The colour is a pale grey

What this means cumulatively is that it is harder to read. So, in the terms that we have been deploying here, that means it is more likely that (conscious, reflective, reasoning, explicit, analytical) System 2 will be switched on.

So, if and when that happens, System 2 is more likely to say the equivalent of, "hang on, hang on, before we rush into anything, let's pause and consider whether it is in fact 10 cents or whether you're going to make us both look stupid."

Hence, the greater chance of arriving at the right answer.

Two implications fall out from this.

First, as we shall see later when we explore framing, a founding precept of classical economics and much of the communications and information world is that the same information is the same information no matter the presentation. But we know in our normal lives that this is false. How information is presented can markedly affect our response to that information.

But my second point is even more ambitious; I'd like to humbly (and rather coyly) offer a global theory of communications.

Why? Because the goal of any communication, especially designed to change behaviour, is to breach 'attention spam.'

This is a term I introduced in *The Storytelling Workbook*, something that emerged serendipitously as a typo. I now use it as a shorthand for comprehensively understanding the goal of any communications to evade the attention spam that our brain is naturally endowed with.

We like to think that everything that we say (or communicate) goes with a smooth inevitability into the warm embrace of the brain's inbox.

But as we have seen, this assumes the brain is a sponge or a computer, and neuroscientists are only too ready to dismiss these. Instead, we must always take our first goal as getting around or through the filtering process known as attention spam.

A (CHEEKY) GLOBAL THEORY OF COMMUNICATIONS

With tongue cheek-adjacent, I'd like to propose the following tri-partite GTC (three being the magic number in storytelling, as regular readers will recall).

If the baseball bat and ball example shows us anything, it is the power of System 2 to intervene. So, let me give what I consider three options for any communications campaign and anyone working on a creative brief or communications strategy.

OPTION A: ALL SYSTEMS GO FOR SYSTEM 1

We are directing our communication primary or exclusively at System 1 because it houses the instincts, drives and desires that we need to reach. System 1 is the secret author and therefore it should be the emotions and drives that are solely the goal of our comms if we seek to change or reinforce behaviour.

OPTION B

A saying I find myself coming back to with alarming frequency, is this from renowned adman, David Ogilvy, "Customers need a rational excuse to justify their emotional decisions. So always include one."

One of the many pearls of words to drop from his lips, this stayed with me for when I was an unformed, baby planner.

What stood out then – and still does – is that word 'excuse.' Not message, benefit, proposition or fact, but *excuse*. Talk about *le mot juste*. It's a word we can all relate to and nails the idea that much, most or all of the time we choose our behaviour based on our emotions and desires, and then seek an excuse afterwards; hence the term 'post-rationalization' – literally meaning to come up with a reason after the event.

As Ogilvy shows us, great communication depends on an emotional drive, but there must be a rational explanation or justification that explains the emotional response that has been excited ("Why am I feeling this disgust? Why do I suddenly feel fear?").

So, start with emotions and System 1 but ensure it is followed by the 'because' of a post-rationalized justification that satisfies fact-checking System 2.

OPTION C

Both of these options may seem uncontroversial, but I would like to give you a third option that brings the baseball bat scenario into play (as it were).

There will be occasions in your strategic and comms life when your goal involves primarily System 2. So, as with the baseball bat, System 2 can play a useful role in pausing System 1's rush to judgment.

If the issue with the brand or the communications is something that exists at an unconscious level – I have always preferred Coke to Pepsi, but don't know why; I have always thought Apple was only for hipsters – then it may need System 2 to be the arm on the shoulder of the precocious yet rigid System 1, in order to pause System 1 and invite it to calmly consider why these attitudes have been so firmly and unsceptically entrenched.

Let me be clear: I am not advocating a return to the 'just put facts out there' approach. But I simply want to suggest a new option where a targeted use of information to question deeply held (and quite possibly unexamined) preconceptions is a viable option.

In most of my comms planning experience since I have posited this theory, the majority of briefs I have written or been involved with have been Option B: attention spam must be breached by emotion, and in its wake comes a rational justification. Next comes Option A – where the goal still remains to use emotions to attract and retain attention. But there have been some occasions where the task is to alert System 2 to something new that might encourage the brain to adjust its opinion (and therefore behaviour).

OUT OF CONTROL

As we said in the introduction and just reminded ourselves, one of our most cherished beliefs is that we are in control of our thoughts.

Let's put that to the test.

Close your eyes.

No, really (if you're skimming the book in a bookshop, don't worry, no one will notice).

Now for five seconds ... don't think of a polar bear.

Tough, eh? Most people are unable to screen out the polar bear, or they do so by thinking of something else (penguins seems to rank quite high). And many people who tell me they didn't conjure up the polar bear, well, I don't want to accuse their unconscious of fibbing but ...

What seems to happen is that System 1 (the secret author ...) hears 'polar bear' and retrieves and throws up an image of the polar bear, despite the instruction that that was precisely the one thing *not* to do. By the time System 2 weighs in and (metaphorically) interjects, "No, no ... he said DON'T think of a polar bear," it's too late.

The late Daniel Wegner,[47] professor of psychology at Harvard, gave credence to the potency of the cognitive unconscious by naming this effect 'ironic process theory.' He describes the tendency to say or do precisely the thing we are trying to avoid when under what psychologists label 'mental load,' such as stress, time pressure, distraction or a bulging inbox.

One of the papers Wegner wrote outlining his theory is worth reading if only for the title: "How to think, say or do precisely the worst thing for any occasion," published in *Science* magazine in 2009.[48]

In the *Science* article, Wegner shows a range of other contexts in which ironic process theory can be found.

For example, sports psychologists and coaches are familiar with 'ironic movement errors': movements that accomplish precisely the opposite of what they are intended to achieve. Wegner cites former major league baseball pitcher Rick Ankiel and his wild throws, which Ankiel called 'the Creature.' Or when putting in golf, the tendency is so prevalent that it has a nickname ('the yips').

Wegner presents evidence from studies that show that golfers who are instructed to avoid a particular error (e.g., "Don't overshoot") are in fact more likely to make that very error when under pressure.

But this is no mere academic theory: it has real-world implications in the comms world.

Two personal examples/anecdotes.

The first (ironically) when I was due to speak on Behavioural Economics at a conference in New York. While on the subway, I spotted a poster for a cocaine addiction clinic, the Columbia University Medical Centre. The headline – "Is cocaine a problem for you? Want help?" – is fairly straightforward. But the image that accompanies the headline is what is so surprising: on the left of the copy and contact information are lines of cocaine (so I'm told). This is a perfect demonstration of what we have been outlining here:

that we think we are talking to the boss (System 2) by showing information, but it's System 1 running the show and the sight of the lines of cocaine is more likely to prompt the exact opposite behaviour (craving for the drug).

The second example ensued from me telling this story at the conference. Afterwards, a delegate approached me and mentioned that she was a marketing professional from a major US university. She told me they had carried out a campaign aimed at reducing levels of smoking among the student body. The marketing team had created a series of large billboard posters, all featuring a giant picture of a cigarette, accompanied by various messages about the dangers of smoking.

We joked that in view of ironic process theory, it was no surprise to hear that after the campaign, levels of smoking had actually *increased*. Why? Because although the messages were directed squarely at System 2, they failed to escape the trap of attention spam ("Stop telling me all this: I am more than familiar with it already and it hasn't changed my behaviour so far"), the close up of a cigarette draws in (sorry) System 1 and makes the desire for a cigarette paramount.

Finally, in September 2021, many social media users in the US started sharing an image of a "Wilmore Funeral Home" truck advertisement that says, "Don't get vaccinated" suggesting that a funeral home was attempting to profit off COVID-19 deaths.[49]

But it turned out that the message wasn't an authentic funeral home promotion, but part of a pro-vaccine campaign designed by local ad agency Boone Oakley. Wilmore Funeral Home was not a real business. Those who clicked on the text were then redirected to the site for a local healthcare provider for COVID-19 testing and vaccinations in Charlotte, North Carolina. The truck drove around downtown Charlotte, and the Bank of America Stadium for a couple of hours on 19 September during a football game.

In a country where vaccine hesitancy was a top concern for health officials, the race to get people in the US vaccinated against the coronavirus and its fast-moving variants spawned an array of advertising campaigns, most of them based on gently convincing people of the proven benefits of the vaccines and the promise of ending the pandemic. (Very System 2).

This ad certainly garnered a lot of attention and the agency heads were clear that they wanted to do something unconventional that would grab attention at a time when lives were at stake from vaccine hesitancy.

I also think Daniel Wegner would have appreciated it too. The "Don't get vaccinated" injunction is a delicious use of ironic process theory, as it goes counter to what is expected, supposedly distributing System 2 advice but startling System 1 into a WTF response.

AUTOMATIC FOR THE PEOPLE
One final point before it is time for all systems gone.

It is in the brain's interest to conserve energy through shortcuts, rapid decisions and all the other processes we have noted. It follows, therefore, that the brain will want to automate as many choices, perceptions and behaviours as it can. So, the brain is constantly and unconsciously involved in a procedure whereby it seeks to take as many things that need attention in System 2 and routinize them to System 1. The term for this is *automaticity*.

Again, let's look at a real-life instance: learning to drive. When we start to learn the skills and operations required to pass a test and qualify to drive on the road, this is System 2-heavy. Lots of taking in facts and procedures, compartmentalizing and remembering them. But once this stage has been accomplished, and the test has been passed, then of course the process of driving becomes natural and automatic (unless you're driving a manual/stick-shift).

Which explains ...

- *Why so much of our communication fails in research or in the marketplace – as it seeks to (only) talk to rational System 2, when System 1 is the power behind the throne.*
- *And why we realize so much of our behaviour is mindless (Why did we eat that entire bucket of popcorn during the movie? How did we drink half that bottle of wine?).*
- *Why learning to drive is so hard, but driving is then effortless.*

So instead, we need to ...

- *Appreciate that emotions come first when designing brands and comms*
- *Think carefully about what approach is best to influence behaviour change using both systems*

PRINCIPLE 3: WHY EMOTION MATTERS

A 1981 paper[50] entitled "A categorized list of emotion definitions, with suggestions for a consensual definition" attempted, as the authors put it, to "resolve the resulting terminological confusion" around the plethora of definitions of emotion. In so doing, it managed to find no less than 92 different definitions of emotion, so I won't attempt to sweep that semantic minefield.

Emotions are best seen as neither rational nor irrational; we just have them, and they are hard to suppress, but let's explore what emotions are and how they work.

Historically the word is relatively modern: some emotion researchers (such as Tiffany Watt Smith) are wont to cheekily propose that we didn't have emotions before 1830, the word emotion being initially proposed by Thomas Brown early in the 19th century. Before then, the most common way of describing what we now call emotions was as passions, accidents of the soul or moral sentiments. In classical Greece, the prevailing theory was the four humours: blood, black bile, choler and phlegm.

STICKS, SNAKES AND BEARS

As we have seen, emotions are complex, largely automated programmes of actions but they have been concocted by evolution to ensure our survival, so they have biological value and biological orientation. They result in a state of altered cognitive resources that adjust our goals and direct our attention and actions.

Emotions lead to the fundamental values of homeostatic regulation, ensuring that we are on an even keel in our fight for survival and fulfilment. Emotions give us information as to reward or punishment, pleasure or pain, whether approach or withdrawal is the preferred option, whether this will lead to personal advantage or disadvantage, or whether this is liable to be good or evil.

Imagine this scenario: one of our distant ancestors has been hunting all day and is bringing the fruits of their hunt back to the tribe for them to savour. It is getting late in the day – perhaps twilight is approaching – and the weight of the animal is adding to the sense of fatigue. There is still some distance to cover to the village, and our hunter is more than aware of the expectation that awaits, so doesn't want to be late.

But then suddenly, out of the corner of their eye, they detect a sudden movement.

So, the issue: what happens next? Because ... it could be a stick, a branch that just fell onto the ground, or it could be the movement of a venomous snake.

Here is where evolution does its work subtly and directly.

What doesn't happen is the following: the hunter delicately lays down the beast, finds the nearest trunk to perch on and engages in a statistical and probabilistic analysis. Well, they ponder in full Rodin's The Thinker mode: statistically the chances are that the sound is that of just another branch or twig falling (they are plentiful). The chances of it being a snake are minimal: when was the last time any of the tribe witnessed a snake (they think: the last person to claim to was Old Ernie, and without casting aspersions, Old Ernie did favour the odd fermented beverage, so wasn't the most reliable source).

So rationally, the answer would be to continue on, get back to the tribe and minimize the disruption and delay.

But this is where evolution chips in. For evolution looks at the big species-wide picture and doesn't care about the maths, the specifics or the detail; evolution operates on the basis of maximizing the fitness of the species, decides that it might be a snake (however low the probability, it won't be zero), so in those interests evolution kicks in and triggers emotions to ensure the survival of that individual.

At the human level, that translates into fear, run and flight. Evolution gets its way.

So, what does this mean in terms of a model of human behaviour? Let's go back to American founding psychologist, William James.

James was the first to elucidate a coherent theory to support the notion that our default theory might be completely topsy-turvy. He theorized that the relationship between emotion and behaviour was, in all likelihood, more complicated, and that in fact, often behaviour might cause emotion rather than the other way round.

In the same way, according to James, smiling can make you feel happy and frowning can make you feel sad. Or, to use James's favourite way of putting it: "You do not run from a bear because you are afraid of it, but rather become afraid of the bear because you run from it."

In evolutionary terms, the relationship between emotion and behaviour described by James makes perfect sense. If evolution designed our emotions to trigger survival responses above everything else, it looks like good design if the first thing we do is carry out the behaviour that will maximize our chances of passing on our genes to future generations.

In the case of danger, that means running first.

The sequence is likely to be:

1. Run ... then ...

2. Experience bodily sensations (elevated heart rate, hair standing on end, sweating) ... then ...

3. Feel the emotion of fear.

The action is triggered first, followed by a bodily signal and finally, as it reaches our conscious awareness, emotion.

Here are some ways of thinking about emotions (as it were).

The traditional theory was that emotions were largely universal (occurring across all cultures, age groups and gender) and innate, with the big six being identifiable through recognizable facial expressions (the so-called facial feedback hypothesis).

The six are generally agreed to be happiness, sadness, fear, anger, surprise and disgust.

Recently, led by professor of psychology at Northeastern University Lisa Feldman Barrett,[51] there has been a reaction against this theory: that maybe emotions are not universal, at least in the sense that not everyone can agree on the consensus of what 'surprise' or 'fear' might look like and, even more crucially for Ekman's theory, that emotions are not simply reactions to the world, but they are constructed.

As an emerging neuroscientist, her insight was based on a failure to replicate experiments that would have validated the dominant theory. So, her first 'botched' experiment seemed to reveal that people often did not distinguish between feeling anxious and feeling depressed. So how reliable were people when they 'saw' surprise, fear or other emotions?

Instead, for Barrett an emotion is your brain's creation of what your bodily sensations mean, and emotional perception is not innate but constructed to both guide our actions and explain to us how we feel. They are not our reactions to the world; they are our constructions of the world. Emotions, as we saw with the stick or snake, become an interpretation of a bodily state. Cordelia Fine sees emotion as a combination of arousal plus emotional thoughts.[52]

So, this is why there is such a close link between emotion and action. Reasoning, it has been said, leads to conclusion: on balance I should stay here, as it's probably a stick; on balance I should go out with that boy tonight.

But emotion has a direct evolutionary link to action: emotion leads to action.

EMOTION, ACTION AND ADVERTISING

So how does this understanding translate into communications and behaviour-change campaigns? Let's look at some examples of effective communications that place emotion first.

Let's start with campaigns devised by the UK's British Heart Foundation (BHF).[53]

The first ad we'll look at was aimed at curbing smoking but was devised to counter the apathy that most people felt towards smoking cessation campaigns: they were conventionally very System 2 focused, full of facts, data, messages and very didactic and perhaps even patronizing in tone. Rightly, the BHF came to realize that this was a failing strategy:

- It fails to hurdle attention spam: the brain sees more of the same and filters (sorry) it out. The primary task of comms failed.

- This is even more so when the same facts, messages and data are parroted (it causes cancer, it will damage your lungs, it will affect your overall health and life expectancy).

- Worse still, the tone of behaviour-change campaigns, especially with cessation goals, tends to be both parent-child, commanding and lacking in empathy with the subject and their behaviour.

"The idea that every cigarette smoked causes fatty deposits to build up in arteries was new to smokers, and something that made them reassess their habit," said Nick Radmore, then head of social marketing and brand at the BHF.

"We also wanted to be seen as the smoker's friend – so we made sure that all of our communications were anti-cigarette, rather than being anti-smoker," added Radmore.

Research conducted after the campaign suggested that 83% felt that it had made them consider quitting smoking.

The second example was based on research by the BHF into snack consumption by young people, which found that among eight- to 15-year-olds, half of children admitted to eating at least one packet of crisps a day, while almost one in five ate crisps twice a day or more. This translated into half of the UK's kids consuming the equivalent of nearly five litres of cooking oil each year.

The poster graphically shows a young girl drinking from a bottle of cooking oil with the headline "What goes into crisps goes into you" to highlight what goes into crisps in a hard-hitting ad campaign by the British Heart Foundation dubbed 'Food4Thought.'

This for me is a crisp (sorry) way of highlighting the power of emotions to lead action, by first gaining attention.

How does it work? By first of all – and before any rational, controlled consciousness can weigh in – creating an emotional response: in this case, that of disgust, one of the big six emotions, whose evolutionary role was originally to ward us off from eating anything that might be poisonous and therefore not in our (or evolution's) interests. That physical disgust is still with us but has also now evolved to be associated with a moral revulsion.

But see how it works in response to the BHF ad: you are viscerally, unconsciously driven by an emotional response to the visual, which you can almost feel pulling on the muscles of your face.

So, in terms that I trust William James would approve of, the sequence here would be:

1. Emotional response, disgust, expressed in the facial muscles.

2. Brain unconsciously alerted by signals that something emotional is happening [System 1], and it's called 'disgust.'

3. Brain sends memo to System 2 to ask for explanation; System 2 decodes disgust signal as "you are feeling this because the fact that crisps contain so much fat is genuinely shocking."

So, the reason I am emphasizing the emotional/System 1 approach is that I believe it is the most successful way of achieving goal 1 – to attract and retain attention.

Which explains ...

- *In most of our behaviour, we know (don't we) that our emotions, impulses and instincts are far more influential than we like to admit: "I really like that Paul Smith jacket and to hell with the cost; I've always wanted to drive a Porsche; I want to be the sort of person who shops at Waitrose."*

So instead, we need to ...

- *Prioritize emotional response first when designing communications.*

PRINCIPLE 4: SOME QUESTIONS FOR MARKET RESEARCH

Let's pause and look specifically at what this means for one of the most crucial components of the marketing system: the practice of market research.

The challenge can be broken down into three components:

1. Our memory is fallible

2. Much of what guides us is not accessible to our consciousness

3. We lack self-insight

Let's unpack these claims and see what they mean for market research.

So, we have observed that we lack control, and with that a large degree of self-awareness or even self-insight.

If System 1 is the secret author of our choices (Kahneman) and the home of our dispositions, traits and temperaments (Wilson), that means that a large portion of what makes us who we are is beyond the reach of our consciousness.

LIES, DAMN LIES AND HOT AIR BALLOONS

MEMORY: VARIABLE CRASHES AND NONEXISTENT BALLOON RIDES

Now add to this the accumulating evidence from various quarters that we are 'unreliable witnesses.'

The human being is a story-telling machine: our self is a story or series of stories that we tell about ourselves to construct our selves.

Let's explore for a moment how our self, our memory and our stories all interweave and overlap, and listen to some insights from one of the most famous living psychologists whose career has been built on demonstrating that our memories are not as perfect as we like to think.

We can begin with a story about US Senator Mitt Romney.

In 2012, Romney gave a speech in Michigan which many found rather moving. In it, he recalled as a child attending the Golden Jubilee, an event that celebrated the 50th year of the automobile. Romney's father was the grandmaster of ceremonies at the event.

A bit of journalistic archaeology uncovered a problem: Romney wasn't actually there. The Golden Jubilee took place on 1 June 1946, which was about nine months before Romney was born.

From the 1960s onwards, Michael Gazzaniga, professor of psychology at UC Santa Barbara, has carried out a number of experiments to explore how our brains create stories to justify our actions (in the trade, this is known as 'confabulation'). Many academic researchers believe it is far more common than we like to admit.

Some people prefer the shorter term: 'lying.'

In one experiment, the word *walk* was presented only to the right side of a patient's brain: as a result, the patient proceeded to get up and start walking. But when he was asked why he did this, his left brain (where language is stored and where the word *walk* was not presented) immediately went into confabulation mode and devised an acceptable reason for the action: "I wanted to go get a Coke."

Before this, a series of fiendishly clever experiments was designed by Elizabeth Loftus, experimental psychologist and currently professor at University of California, Irvine and the highest-ranked woman in the top 100 living psychological researchers of the 20th century in 2002.[54]

She had already outlined her view of memory as far slipperier and more malleable than was the current orthodoxy and had been involved in controversial trials, including an early incident featuring Ted Bundy. But after her failure to defend a father who had been accused of a horrific act by his daughter and the outpouring of 'false memory' incidents in the US, she decided to create a scientific means of demonstrating the extent to which our memory can be shaped and contaminated.

One famous study demonstrated the power of priming and framing on the memory: Loftus's team showed subjects a clip of a car crash and then asked them how fast the car was going when it hit (or smashed or collided into) the other car. Estimates varied wildly depending on the verb used, suggesting that leading questions can distort and contaminate memory. This led her to ask whether it would be possible to implant entirely false memories.

In one of these studies, she persuaded family members of her subjects to write three genuine accounts of childhood memories of the subject, plus one that was fictitious, about being lost in a shopping mall, being found by a kind older woman, before being retrieved by their parents. About one in four fell for this and confabulated both in depth and time. The implanted memories had great durability, besides. A week later, they would return to Loftus's team and embellish more detail into the false memory: the lady was wearing an unusual hat, my mother was so mad ... so, she discovered that not only is it possible to implant entirely new memories in the brain, but we naturally embrace and embroider them, unknowingly weaving a thread of fantasy and truth that becomes impossible to disentangle.

More recently a team from New Zealand convinced family members (they seemed only too happy to comply) to fake a picture of a hot-air balloon incident. Again, when interviewed, about a third of the guinea pigs claimed they could recall the incident and even managed to describe it with some richness. The paper they wrote was memorably titled "A picture is worth a thousand lies."[55, 56]

More specifically (and worryingly for those who like to maintain the purity myth of memory), there is ample evidence that information that is acquired after an event can significantly alter the memory of that event. The process of retrieval and filling in means that not every telling of an event will be the same, or that the copying fidelity will be as high as we'd like to think. Loftus constantly reiterates her astonishment at the detail that we confabulate and then believe, and what Lauren Slater calls the 'confusion between imagination and memory.'

As Loftus said about Romney:

"When we remember something, we're taking bits and pieces of experience – sometimes from different times and places – and bringing it all together to construct what might feel like a recollection but is actually a construction. The process of calling it into conscious awareness can change it, and now you're storing something that's different. We all do this, for example, by inadvertently adopting a story we've heard – like Romney did."

RE-WEAVE NOT RETRIEVE

Scientists have gathered much evidence (again, crucially, from literature as well as science) to conclude that we should stop thinking of remembering as a passive process of calling up a stored fact and printing it out. Rather than merely pulling a document from a file manager, we should return to the etymology of 'remember,' with its implication of 'assembling,' 'connecting' and the brain's active participation in the process.

Harvard psychology professor Daniel Gilbert[57] exposed some of the weaknesses of our thinking systems and our inability to forecast our emotional states. He also shows how the brain creates illusions to fill in gaps, and how:

"... the elaborate tapestry of our experience is not stored in its entirety but is compressed. So that later when we want to recall that experience, our brains re-weave the tapestry by fabricating, not by actually retrieving."

As someone who has written on storytelling and the importance of a Golden Thread, I can't help but admire the metaphor he uses here.

THE PROBLEM FOR MARKET RESEARCH

This poses immense problems for the practice of market research, which has been largely predicated on the basis of asking people questions: about their behaviour (past, present and future/likely) and their perceptions and attitudes.

The essence of market research as a tool of marketing is to provide answers about consumer behaviour and inform decisions in the light of those findings and insights. The founding philosophy of market research is grounded in asking questions.

So, what happens if we (and let's not think of it as 'they', please) are simply unable to answer those questions?

In the past, as ad planners and users of research, we were often warned that respondents may not "tell the truth," either because they were not prepared to share the truth with researchers or there were social factors precluding them from being honest; this was especially prevalent in political polling.

But with the arrival of Behavioural Economics, conventional market research has been subjected to even deeper analysis as disquiet deepened about the promise of market research to deliver what was asked of it (it didn't help that many brands found out – often painfully – that people didn't seem to actually do in reality what they had promised in the research forum, and many brands, or their ad campaigns, suffered from that mismatch).

Because as BE practitioners noted, if human beings are notoriously unreliable witnesses, that opens the door to the possibility that a large portion of our market research is futile.

That is why we have friends, family and even therapists, as other people to see ourselves through.

Two social psychologists meet in the street.

"Hi, you're fine. How am I?"

Or in the words of Scottish poet Rabbie Burns:[58]

*"O wad some power the giftie gie us
To see oursels as ithers see us."*

Take estate agents, or realtors in the US. I was at another US event talking about BE and covering this point about lack of self-insight, when a US realtor approached me to share with me an industry truth. We have a saying, she said, that "buyers lie." That when buyers come to realtors, they have a series of requirements or desires for a property, but that often these turn out not to be unexpectedly flexible. UK readers will be familiar with a TV series called *Location, Location, Location*. Named after the estate agents' mantra, it is a British primetime property programme that has aired on Channel 4 since 2000.

It occurs not infrequently on this show that buyers are asked for their house-hunting priorities, and then they are shown several options that fit their guidelines. But it is often the case that the presenters will throw in a wild-card option that differs from the hunters' specifications. And, yes, in a significant minority of those cases, people will choose the wild-card option. Which is odd, given it was not what they themselves had explicitly desired.

Moral: not only do we often not know what we want, but we don't know what it is till we see it. The implications for research are profound: when asking people hypothetical questions about their likely or future plans, intentions or propensities, we must be extra cautious, as our reactions to hypotheses ("How likely would you be to buy this new yogurt?") are often just System 2 filling in, or confabulation.

Showing the real thing in an authentic context is the best way of achieving a more realistic and helpful outcome.

RESEARCHING UNRELIABLE WITNESSES

Here are some tips and reminders that anyone commissioning or conducting market research (or involved in any business that uses it) should bear in mind before they start, in order to understand consumer behaviour and design communication against it.

1. Not relying on System 2:

- Be very wary that if you are conducting any research (qualitative as well as more obviously quantitative), you may be limiting yourself to (logical, rational, factual) System 2-type questioning. These answers may not be wrong as such, but it is important to accept their limitations. If you fail to access System 1 ('the secret author'), then you are missing out on what are, in all probability, the real motivators and drivers, reactions and feelings that your brand or communication depend on.

2. Exploring System 1 research approaches:

- It follows, then, that you should find ways of accessing System 1. By definition this is tricky, as normal questioning cannot really get to System 1.

- There are glimmers of hope for clients wanting to get to System 1's riches. In qualitative research and some quantitative, it has long been a tried-and-tested option to use projective techniques to allow respondents to respond creatively and indirectly (using pictures, projection techniques, "If the brand were a car, what car would it be ... "). My own favourite approach is to invite stories and anecdotes rather than factual Q&As.

- But some companies are beginning to explore more dedicated approaches that home in on System 1. One particular technique is based on IATs – Implicit Attitude (or Association) Testing. This has been used especially in big corporations to help employees recognize their unconscious bias. People are shown images and associations at subliminal level at great speed and are invited to make quick-fire responses.

- This can obviate the need for rational explicit messaging or associations ("When you think of Snickers, what sort of snack-based eating occasions come to mind?") and replace it with something that works at hyper-fast speeds and at a latent level with System 1 (in other words, before the voice of reason and rationalization, System 2, can get involved). With IATs, the speed indicates the strength of the association: what is more readily and rapidly associated together is a measure of the depth of that association.

3. Comparing what S2 and S1 say:

- Less of a warning and injunction, more some helpful advice if you are seeking insight from your research (and who isn't?). Some of the most helpful insights I have witnessed or fallen upon have come from comparing what people in research *say* they do or believe, with what *seems to be* the case when you ask them indirectly.

- I worked with a client in the butter market (still jargonistically called 'yellow fats') and heard all the traditional research. In the conventional research we had commissioned, we heard all sorts of rationalizations for people choosing the brand leader.

4. Hot Cold Empathy Gap:

- This brings us to something known as the Hot Cold Empathy Gap.[59] In the language favoured by jobbing psychologists, "people mispredict their affective states." When people are in a cold (unemotional) state, we tend to under-appreciate the effect of 'hot' states on our behaviour.

- For example, in a hot state we tend to assume we are acting more dispassionately than we actually are. This is the cause of many crimes of passion, for example. In the opposite 'cold' state, (or not 'affectively aroused,' to use the technical term), it becomes hard to imagine how we would react if we were subject to thirst, hunger, fear or pain. So just as we may be unable to imagine how we ourselves would think and behave in the other state, the same applies for our expectations of other people.

- Either way, it reminds us that we constantly overestimate the stability of our preferences and forget that those preferences can – and often do – change in different circumstances.
- George Loewenstein, a professor of economics and psychology at Carnegie Mellon, carried out much of the research in this area, specifically with regards to medical decision-making and cancer treatment: he found that the Hot Cold Empathy Gap meant that some healthy patients could expose themselves to unhealthy outcomes, and that healthcare providers are liable to underestimate patients' pain. This is no mere abstract psychological finding, but bears on many elements of marketing, and especially market research.
- As we saw, market research that relies on asking people questions (we will come back to that again later) depends on people having accurate access to their actions, memories and likely future behaviour. But too often I have observed that we ignore the impact of the Hot Cold Empathy Gap in at least two ways.
- First, asking people in one state about their past or (especially) likely future behaviour in another.
- I used to be the (strategic) planner working at an agency on an account for a large cruise company. They wanted to ask existing and past cruisers how they felt about cruising, their brand, their ships, destinations, etc. and suggested we do a typical focus group, recruiting respondents to a venue, such as a hotel. But my feeling was that this would not get the depth of insight we were seeking. Why? Because a room in a hotel in Manchester or Ealing is a context that is 'cold' (with due apologies

to some undoubtedly inviting accommodation hotels in both those places): this makes the context rather impersonal, being surrounded by strangers and invited to ponder the joys and wonders of cruising, in an environment that is wholly alien to the act of being on a cruise. It was trying to understand a fundamentally hot situation (A ship! The sea! A plethora of destinations! Twenty-four-hour food!) in a cold context.

- My recommendation was to carry out the research on the ship itself: this would avoid the Hot Cold Empathy Gap, as it would ensure people were in the right context, mood and state when giving their answers to questions relating to cruising. Fortunately, the client agreed, and the data we got back was (I hope) far more illuminating than other work we had previously done in 'cold' hotel rooms. *(The fact that this meant I had four days on a cruise ship myself was completely incidental.)*

- The second element, if you are unable to change the context of the research in this way, is to consider the mood that you create around the research situation. If you are unable for logistical reasons to place respondents in the heat of the 'hot' state, do consider how you might be artificially able to recreate that state. In my cruising example, had we not had the chance to research on board, we could have thought of ways to at least heat up the state of the room to mimic the cruising experience: showing videos of the sea, posting pictures on the wall of different destinations, mealtimes, displaying the daily schedule of onboard events.

5. **Other types of research.** This includes semiotics, the study of signs and symbols, appreciating the importance of encoding and decoding meaning in brands and communication.

Which explains:

- *Why so many brands fail when listening unthinkingly to what people say in market research.*
- *Because we all know that often we can give an answer to questions such as, "Why do you shop at Tesco? Why do you vote for this party? Why do you choose Coke and not Pepsi?" and we give an answer that we think makes us look good, or we can't actually remember, or System 2 is the cause of System 1's choice – but it's only a guess.*

So instead, we need to ...

- *Find ways of using market research – or observation – to explore these emotional wellsprings of choice.*

PRINCIPLE 5: WE ARE SOCIAL ANIMALS

"When people are free to do as they please, they usually imitate each other."

Eric Hoffer, American moral and social philosopher[60]

The next cherished self-belief under the microscope is that we are wholly independent and autonomous units of reasoning, untainted by the opinions of others.

It is easy to see why evolution wants us to feel or experience the sense of autonomy and agency, a sense of untethered consciousness and free will.

But again, not much revisionism is required to realize that our pretended level of independence is largely a sham. Social psychologists have known for decades that we are far more ruled by the effects of compliance and conformity than we might wish to acknowledge or declare.

Let's start with one famous example (there is voluminous literature, many experiments being so well-known as almost to be part of the pop-psychology book canon).[61]

After World War II, many social psychologists (a number of whom were Jewish émigrés from Germany) sought explanations for the widespread support for Nazism. The influence of the Holocaust was profound in the development of the new science of social psychology, pioneered by the likes of Kurt Lewin, Serge Moscovici, Henri Tajfel and Stanley Milgram (best known now for his obedience experiments).

With the horrors of WWII fresh in their minds, people were shocked at the ease with which ordinary soldiers seemed to be capable of the most barbaric atrocity simply because they were doing what the majority was doing: just 'following orders.' This fear of conformity was fuelled when, at the height of the Cold War, reports emerged suggesting that American prisoners of war were being brainwashed by the communists: the POWs would seem to be denouncing American capitalism, appearing to fully embrace the communist cause. What seemed even more troubling was the fact that it did not appear to take all that much for these soldiers to take the side of their captors.

One of the leading lights of this group was Solomon Asch (Polish born, but who emigrated to the States at the age of 13), who in 1951 devised the 'line judgment' study to explore the nature and extent of social conformity.

The experimental procedure he devised was as follows.

A number of students were recruited for what they were told was a vision test (one of the issues with many of these famous/notorious experiments is that they tread a thin line ethically, as they depend at least to some degree on deception).

Each respondent was shown a 'target' line, then shown a range of three lines and asked to guess which of the three was the same length as the target line. There were eight people in the room, but seven were 'stooges' or confederates of Asch, who were in on the experiment. The subjects completed 18 trials. For the first two trials, both the subject and the confederates gave the obvious, correct answer. On the third trial, the actors would all give the same wrong answer.

In the control group situation (with no pressure to conform), less than 1% would give the wrong answer. But on average, about one third (32%) of the participants who were placed in this situation went along and conformed with the (clearly incorrect) majority on the critical trials. Over the trials, about 75% of participants conformed at least once showing that we will go against what we (objectively, rationally, System 2-ly) know to be the truth in order to fit with others. (Those in search of a movie reference can look to the Marx Brothers *Duck Soup,* where Chico – disguised as Groucho – quips to Margaret Dumont: "Who you gonna believe – me or your own eyes?")[62]

The legacy of Asch's experiments has been profound. Asch-style conformity has been argued to underlie behaviours as diverse as war crimes, eating disorders and football hooliganism. And another marker of Asch's influence is a more personal one: Stanley Milgram, whose obedience experiments have also become a seminal part of the conformity literature, worked under Asch; Asch was Milgram's advisor at Princeton University, and Milgram completed his dissertation on national differences in conformity under Asch.

Milgram's work further demonstrates the power of compliance and the degree to which a person's own opinions are influenced by those of a group: we will go to almost any lengths (even savagery against strangers) to obey authority and conform.[63]

One of my favourite demonstrations of the power of social conformity is what I suppose we now have to call a meme: a Christmas decoration of a 'ditto' sign, pointing at a neighbour's more traditionally gaudy Christmas lighting display.[64]

It is wryly amusing, mildly critical and also reminds us of the power of effortlessness.

Another choice example is from a 1962 episode of the US series *Candid Camera*, featuring a stunt in an elevator, called "Face the Rear."[65]

For the subjects of *Candid Camera*'s elevator gag, where subjects willingly change positions to fit in with the prank by the team, the pressure to succumb to groupthink quickly overruled years of learned physical behaviour. And this was no mere comic prank: its creator, Allen Funt, was well versed in psychology, having served as psychologist Kurt Lewin's research assistant at Cornell University.

APPLICATION OF SOCIAL CONFORMITY

Referred to diversely as social norms, social proof, behaviour cascades or emotional contagion, this principle has been one of the earliest and most widespread of BE principles to have been adopted by those involved in behaviour change, from governments downwards.

In *Predictably Irrational*,[66] Israeli-American professor of psychology and Behavioural Economics Dan Ariely talks of 'herding' and self-herding as:

"When we assume that something is good or bad on the basis of other people's previous behaviour and our own actions follow suit. ...'self-herding' [is] when we believe something is good or bad on the basis of our own behaviour and follow the same decisions we have made in the past – we become the second person in line standing behind ourselves."

Let's examine some real-life applications of the social conformity/ norming principle.

SOCIAL NORMS FOR STUDENTS

When I was working with the UK government on an anti-bullying campaign, I discovered an initiative carried out by the Hobart and William Smith College, a private liberal arts college in Geneva, New York.

The Alcohol Education Project[67] was established by them to better inform students, faculty and staff in higher education and secondary school settings about alcohol and other drugs and related social norms to help address problems of abuse.

This remains a very useful resource for collating various campaigns that have been created, specifically using social norms approaches rather than more conventional "don't smoke/drink/take drugs it's bad" angle.

Some of the posters have had the school's name changed, but the messages used include:

- "Did you know that ...": most Cooper Middle school students (eight out of ten) think that students should tell a teacher or counsellor if they or someone else are being bullied at school.

- "You told us ..." campaign: including "You told us that 83% of us feel that tobacco use is never a good thing" or "Most Colorado High School students have not consumed alcohol in the last month."

- "Look around ...": the majority of us do not use tobacco.

- "Join the crowd ...": 86% of us have never used marijuana.

- "Cooper Middle School students make GREAT CHOICES ...": most Cooper Middle School students (three out of four) do not exclude someone from a group to make them feel bad.

- "Strength in Numbers ...": just the facts.

- "Be proud, join the crowd ...": most Rochester families are strong; 81% of Roc families help and support each other.

- "Don't tell me NOT to do something I'm not already doing ...": seven out of ten Summit High School students don't drink in an average week. This is us. We're better than you think.

These all draw from the same well.

They are not demonizing the social issue or patronizing the audience, but provide data-based evidence that the specific behaviour is not that common and therefore not something that should be widely and specifically imitated. If the norm is not to drink, that is the norm that you should adhere to.

There are specific differences, too:

- Many deploy inclusive language that reinforces the norming effect: join the crowd, strength in numbers.

- Some use more questioning techniques: "Did you know that ...?" As we have said with our storytelling hat on, the interrogative perspective (asking a question) is an effective way of getting through attention spam, as when System 1 is faced with a question it cannot but want to find the answer.

- Some, though, do apply the imperative ("Look around ...") but feel less pushy and instructional.

- There is a lot of reinforcement in these ideas, too: "You make great choices" feels reassuring rather than persecutory. "You told ..." also plays into the feeling that this is being led by the audience rather than those in authority.

- And the last one does something even more original. First, there is ironic process theory going on ("Don't tell me ...") with a tone of voice that feels very right for the adolescent target group. But it also oozes attitude and pride: "We're better than you think," which feels like another way of bolstering a common identity among this notoriously tribal age group.

SOCIAL COMPARISON FOR ENERGY USE

One of the defining examples of BE and social norms being used as a nudge in the commercial realm was devised by Opower, a company whose goal was to help millions of people save energy. But rather than selling or producing energy, it made software.[68]

From its founding, the company had teamed up with energy producers to monitor customers' energy consumption. Their insight was that not only is energy consumption considered to be relatively low interest, but the form the information takes doesn't help.

So, they helped transform the existing information you get from your energy bill into a real-time reminder of your energy use, but to then take it a step further by using the power of social comparison to activate social norms.

This approach was influenced by, (as it were) among others, the King of Influence, Robert Cialdini, professor of psychology and marketing and author of *Influence: The Psychology of Persuasion*.[69]

In addition to showing a household's energy use, the monthly energy report included a bar graph that compared that household's own energy consumption with the community's average; but a third bar displayed that of the community's most energy-efficient households. One other – by no means minor – element: a smiley emoticon/grade assessing your energy consumption. You received two smiley faces for the best conservation (using less than 80% of what your neighbours do), one for good (using less than most of your neighbours do) and none for bad (using more than most of your neighbours).

This works at three levels:

- The smiley face gives an immediate sense of reward and gratification.

- The comparison bars have social incentive to strive to keep up with or exceed the Joneses.

- There is a component of progress monitoring showing how your consumption has changed over time.

An analysis carried out of the effectiveness of this approach with a control group that received the standard report showed that the Opower method reduced consumption by around 2%, which equated to one billion pounds (over 450,000 tonnes) of CO^2-emission, the equivalent of $75 million in energy savings.

UK GOVERNMENT AND COVID-19

For our third example, we can look at how the UK government created a massive behaviour-change campaign in the midst of the COVID pandemic to 'act like you've got the virus' at the heart of the spread of the virus, in January 2021, in order to 'flatten the curve.'[70]

The standpoint of the government was to focus on the NHS (National Health Service), which they were concerned could buckle under the pressure of the pandemic, as infection rates across the entire country continued to soar at an alarming rate. With the new variant spreading quickly across the country, the scientists and politicians realized that this put many people at risk of serious disease and was placing a lot of pressure on the NHS. Along with a national lockdown, a new campaign was rolled out with the slogan *"Stay at home. Protect the NHS. Save lives."*

My aim here is not to become involved in the politics or even the strategy the government chose, but merely to delve into how they applied social norms to the campaign they introduced. Being well-versed in 'nudge' theory and with the resources of a dedicated and experienced Behavioural Insights team, this social-norms approach would have been an obvious line of attack in the behaviour-change arena.

As well as using the magic number three (see *The Storytelling Workbook*), this is a classic application of social norms. It does have a direct and exhortatory feel (three verbs in the imperative) but at its heart is the exertion of social pressure to collectively conform, with all the attendant threat to those who opt out or try to cheat the system.

IMPLICATIONS

Despite what we have said about targeting System 1 rather than the rational/logical System 2, BE does not have to be the implacable enemy of data.

Many of these examples do use data very directly and systematically.

What they don't do is bludgeon the viewer with reams of statistics, focusing on one substantive point, followed by another message using the same process.

Neither do they use the language that is often common to campaigns aimed at social or behavioural change: the very teacherly, didactic and – frankly – often patronizing tone, frequently adopted in an adult-to-child/adolescent manner by groups in positions of authority. There is little moralizing or sermonizing.

Which explains ...

- *Why, as social animals, so often we aren't as independent as we'd like to believe. We follow fashions, not just in clothes, but in ideas and culture, from Crocs to conspiracies.*

So instead, we need to ...

- *Don't assume we only talk to individuals in marketing and comms. Think about how to create emotional contagion for your brand and think about tribal behaviour, too.*

PRINCIPLE 6: CHOICE ARCHITECTURE AND FRAMING

THE ONLY WAY IS ETHICS

I often kick off my training workshops by inviting attendees to answer a simple but playful and eye-opening question: "What did your parents think or hope you would be when you were little?"

(One of my favourite answers was, "I was given four choices as a child: doctor, lawyer, accountant or a disgrace to the family.")

When I occasionally get asked, "Well, what about you?" one answer I favour is "architect," as I spent a large part of my youth playing with Lego. This was enough to convince my parents that they had birthed a potential Frank Lloyd Wright or Richard Rodgers. Disappointingly for them, I then discovered chemistry, before disposing with test tubes, Bunsen burners (and ... yes ... asbestos mats) and discovering Latin and Greek. But even having studied that at school and university, I continued to baffle them by making the obvious move into a career in advertising.

But the only connection with my first likely profession is belatedly finding myself acting, in the words of Richard Thaler and Cass Sunstein of *Nudge* fame, as a 'choice architect.'

The *Nudge* guys popularized this term to suggest that those operating in the behaviour-change world (especially – their prime concern – at the government/public sector level) have the opportunity (maybe even the duty) to nudge people to carry out behaviours that will be to their advantage, even if they are unaware of their benefits.

They called it 'benign paternalism,' which doesn't exactly dispel the spectre of a governmental Big Brother forcing/coercing us (under the rather jollier term of 'nudging') to do what that government (political party, faction, special interest group, lobby) thinks is right for us.

Ethics is a major topic for those operating in the field of Behavioural Economics, but it should hardly be a shock. Advertising (as it used to be known) has always operated at the level of the emotions, and ever since qualitative research and researchers in general became widespread (Ernest Dichter was the figurehead), understanding the deepest (truest) desires of human beings has been at the centre of great insight, communications and branding. Whether you call it manipulating, persuading, coercing or anything even more pejorative, Behavioural Economics in many senses is not that new, but merely a codification and validation of many insights and creative perspectives that seem to work in the marketplace.

Let's explore two complementary aspects here: what is choice architecture, and the creatively liberating perspective known as framing (or reframing).

Let's begin with exploring what choice architecture is and, more importantly, what it leads to.

ARCHITECTS ASSEMBLE!

Anyone who grew up with the bible of positioning (by Ries and Trout) or experienced training in the basics of marketing, will recall the emphasis of owning a position, defending it with large budgets and fending off your rivals from grabbing your position. The assumption was that 'consumers' were making rational and logical evaluations of brands, categorizing them neatly and rationally.

I remember it led to lots of rational messages and benefits and a seemingly clinical obsession with image batteries, statements and an almost chess-like approach to communication.

Let's see what Behavioural Economics might add to this picture.

Here are some of the tenets of choice architecture:

1. There is no neutral way to present a choice.
   - One of the presumptions of the logical positioning model is that it exists in a consumer's mind, and is unchanging and consistent. But one of the principles of choice architecture is that context can be a game-changing determinant: how a choice is structured is far more important than we sometimes acknowledge. If people are offered a choice of chicken or beef, a certain number will choose beef. If you expand the choice to be chicken, beef or lamb, that choice is differently structured and perceived by the brain – suddenly there are two red meat choices. The context crucially affects how we see each choice, not just the individual evaluation of benefits, pros and cons.

2. People choose according to what is available rather than what they want.

   • Again, what we were told was that people will go out of their way to make the best choice that they can (remember maximizing their utility from earlier?). But as we have seen, Daniel Kahneman, among others, pointed out that the brain's desire for *effortlessness* means that we will often err on the side of what is available: the lightly technical term meaning that we tend to rely over-heavily on information or signals that are immediately at hand. Kahneman labelled this WYSIATI ('what you see is all there is').

3. This is why brand owners often assume too much (System 2) mindedness, concentration and effort on the part of their users (or nonusers), rather than System 1 going for what is easy and available. This is why brand owners need to consider context, comparisons, similarities and dissimilarities.

SOME EXAMPLES

Nick Chater, professor of behavioural science at Warwick Business School, gives this example of 'apples and pears.' Take a range of instant coffee jars – on average, 5p a cup. Then take your favourite coffee house – around £2.50/£3 for the equivalent. It's easy to compare brands of instant coffee, but not instant coffee with Starbucks in terms of their absolute value. This reminds us of the age-old question to always ask clients: Exactly what business are you in? Are you in the quick convenience market, the taste market, or are you in the conspicuous-consumed leisure moment market, or what? Beware thinking only of your own direct competitors, because human beings don't.

I used to work on the ad account for KFC (don't judge me; I had small children to support). For an awayday workshop where pushing the envelope out of the box was the goal, we tried out a new way of asking "Exactly what business are you in?" using concentric circles.

The inner, closest circle was generally agreed (by the client anyway) to be 'fried chicken outlets.'

Next out was typically fast-food restaurants (which the industry prefers to call QSRs – quick service restaurants); one circle beyond and you look at other casual dining outlets that people may visit, especially in their lunch breaks.

And then?

We landed on "15 minutes of your lunch break." From this, it was a short step to popcorn chicken.

THE FRAME GAME

Framing is defined as the expression of logically equivalent information (whether numerical or verbal) in different ways.[71]

Framing owes much of its fame to two Israeli scientists, Daniel Kahneman and his partner Amos Tversky (who sadly passed away in 1996). Under the heading of Prospect Theory, they outlined the academic groundwork for framing that those in the comms business had been using without the theoretical validation. But now that we are fully armed with the power of framing, we should explore its impact.

In Kahneman and Tversky's terms, the framing effect operates when an individual's choice from a set of options is influenced more by how the information is presented than by the information itself. The framing of an issue, whether presented in a positive (gain-oriented) or negative (loss-oriented) light, can significantly impact how people perceive and therefore make decisions. This also ties into what they called 'loss aversion' – the fact that the brain hates losing far more than it likes winning,

Before we look at the comms world, we can spend a moment looking at how it has been used in the broader arena, starting with the medical and legal domains.

1. One of the seminal papers by K&T was an analysis of framing in the medical world. Participants were presented with a classic framing effect problem, referred to as the 'Asian Disease' design. A simpler version is one where people are given two options: with one medical treatment, there is a 90% chance they will survive after five years; in the alternative option, they are told they have a 10% chance of dying after five years.

    Significantly more subjects opt for the first option.

    Which is odd, as they are, of course, precisely the same information, but presented in different ways.

    The first is framed (and decoded) in a much more positive light. The semantic frame is of survival (generally considered a good thing) and 90% is a healthily robust number; in the second case, however, the semantic mood is one of death (never good) and the 10% indicates a less likely choice. Again, as we saw earlier, classical economists (and many people in the communications world) think the equivalence is total: it is (rationally, computationally, in System 2 world) identical. But we know (don't we) that they are definitely not processed in the same way.

In another medical example, patients were offered a choice: a hip replacement (surgery) or medication.[72] In that case, 47% chose the medication. But when patients were offered two alternative types of medicine, only 28% (in total) chose either form of medication. Why? Because as with the chicken-beef-lamb choice, you are suddenly confronted with two levels of choice: surgery or medication, but then which type of medication? And then the brain often finds it easier to make just one choice rather than two.

2. Framing effects have also been shown to influence legal proceedings. A paper written in 2004 by Stephanos Bibas,[73] a US law professor and judge, examined how framing influenced plea bargains in legal trials. Bibas argued that defendants were less likely to accept plea bargains because they regarded them through a 'loss frame.' In other words, because defendants were used to being free, and were being faced with a loss of freedom in a plea bargain – even if it is a lesser loss than a conviction without a plea bargain – they were still more likely to resist bargaining. Defendants seeing through a loss frame viewed acquittal as the baseline, and anything worse than this was therefore a loss. Bibas believes this benefits prosecutors, as defendants often stand to gain from concessions and bargaining.[67]

We are now inured to seeing this in our normal world of purchasing and perceiving. One of the classical examples carried out in the academic world, but that feels self-evidently familiar to us, examined features of meat described as being 25% fat or as 75 % lean (Levin and Gaeth). The description of 75% lean meat (in a positive frame) was judged more desirable than the negatively framed description of 25% fat meat.

FRAMING IN ACTION

Let's explore more examples of framing to remind ourselves of its power and versatility. Much will revolve around food and drink, so I recommend you are fully sated before you start this section.

Would Sir/Madam like the second-cheapest wine?

The typical restaurant-goer will accept that we normally avoid choosing the cheapest wine on the menu, usually because one doesn't want to appear cheap (especially if we are trying to impress someone). We may veil this with a veneer of quality, but by and large that is our reaction. Instead, we opt for the second-cheapest wine as the safer option. But restaurants know the power of framing, so they place the wine they will make the most profit on second or third from the bottom (fun fact).

Or take the perception of a £20 bottle of wine. (This comparison has been tested out frequently in the academic literature.) If it is the most expensive on the wine list, our perception is that it should taste la crème de la crème; however, if on another wine list it appears midway down the table (a sort of Crystal Palace of the wine world), then we expect it to be middling.

So far, so obvious, you may interject. But when this is tested out in research, not only does the perceptual ranking play out as we expect, but that is how people respond to the *taste* of the wine in each scenario: they claim that in the first case the wine tastes like it has earthy balance and a zesty backbone with legs, but in the second version, they are more likely to claim it to be flabby plonk.

So, framing is far more far-reaching than it appears at first sip. The latter result shows that framing alters not just perception but reality. In the case of the wine (six bottles to the case?), the framing creates the expectation so that we do not taste *reality*, we taste *expectation*.

Next, an example that focuses on soda drinks in the US and the attempts to encourage people to make healthier choices with their food and drink. In 2013, then-mayor of New York, Michael Bloomberg, sought to impose a sugary drinks portion cap; this soda ban was a proposed limit on soft drink size in New York City, intended to prohibit the sale of any sweetened drinks more than 16 fluid ounces (0.47 litres) in volume.[74]

There was already plenty of data to show that portion sizes had increased over the last 30 years and childhood obesity rates had tripled. For a 2011 paper in the *Journal of Nutrition*,[75] Carmen Piernas and Barry Popkin used national surveys to study the diets of more than 30,000 kids and measure how their 'junk-food' habits had changed from 1977 to 2006. They found that soft drink portions had increased by almost one-third. (Once upon a time, a 'king-size soft drink' was just 12 ounces.)

But one study was especially revealing in what we are showing with the power of framing. In not dissimilar fashion to the 'second cheapest wine,' we will view a 32-ounce fizzy drink differently according to the context or range that it is placed in: when the 32 ounce is the second-largest super-size option (the biggest being, say 44 ounces) there is 15% more consumption of the 32-ounce portion compared to when the 32-ounce size itself is the largest available. This is readily explained (post-rationalized) as, "Well, it could have been worse."

So again, we see the power or range and context to affect choice, which goes well beyond the narrow parameters of positioning, product differentiation, etc.

BRAND REFRAMING

1. Häagen Dazs

One of the best-known case histories for launching a luxury brand in the middle of a recession, in the 1990s, the goal of Häagen Dazs was to create a new type of ice cream and break the category norms that ice cream was cheap and mainly for families and children.

Häagen-Dazs UK decided to use the London ad agency Bartle, Bogle and Hegarty (BBH), best known at the time for the Levi 501s advertising, and set them the brief to help Häagen-Dazs create a new 'gold standard' to become the ultimate ice cream in the market.

The goal was a super-premium brand that was a 'sensual pleasure': the tagline was "dedicated to pleasure," accompanied by relatively steamy 'adult' imagery. In 1991, the launch campaign ensured it became the most talked about ice cream brand in the country.

This is one of the great examples of a strategic success coming from reframing out of the conventional category definitions.

2. Airline profits

One of my favourite examples I came across on X (or ex-Twitter), which I believe was shown at a Global Travel Summit in 2019.

The poster has a massive visual of a burger (Big Mac); on the left, the statement "$6.12 profit per passenger"; on the right, "$6.62 price of a Big Mac in Switzerland."[76]

What a brilliantly insightful and revelatory way of reframing what could be a dry piece of data and taking it out of its usual environment. The desire to shock by showing how little profit the airline industry was making is beautifully crafted to gain maximum impact with the minimum of cognitive effort.

3. Burgers reframed as office supplies

Still on burgers, a recent example from the Toronto Good Fortune Burger restaurant also caught my eye for the cheek involved if nothing else.[77]

While most items on this restaurant's menu have 'normal' names (like the Fortune Burger), the restaurant launched a limited-time #Receats (or receipts) menu on food delivery services such as Uber Eats and DoorDash that included renamed menu items as office supplies so workers could expense them. So, 'ergonomic aluminium laptop' was code for the Double Your Fortune Burger and 'wired earphones with Mac' was the Emerald Veggie Burger (surely should have been Apple Mac and Cheese?). Though designed purely to bring a smile to people's faces, we commend them for their savvy reframing.

4. Dine in …

An in-store promotion for UK retailer Marks and Spencer's food a few years back (before the current cost-of-living crisis) offered "Dine in for two – £10."

A very simple piece of framing at the semantic level. The words 'dine in' explicitly raise a meaning in your brain – a context of 'not dine out' or 'dining in' (at home). In that comparison, £10 for two people is undoubtedly great value ("We couldn't eat out in a restaurant for that price").

Without that reference, merely saying "A meal for two people for £10" would sound much more humdrum and less attractive.

5. Trojan of course

Whether a genuine in-store ad/promotion, or an amusing prank, this became something of a meme.[78] On a shelf selling Trojan condoms at one level and Huggies diapers/nappies beneath, some wit has attached a semi-official-looking notice:

Compare and Save:
Trojan Condoms $3.25
Huggies Diapers $22

Again, kudos to whoever devised this (professional comms expert or gifted amateur). What a smart way of drawing attention to the cost of childcare, especially if that's not what you have in mind, and making the cost of condoms look suddenly like a very good long-term value.

6. Chalk board and cheese

A personal instance here, found when in a gift shop at a stately home in England. On sale, small chalkboards that were used in UK schools in previous times, but they were positioned as 'Victorian iPads.' Neat.

7. Rolls Royce

One of the most memorable examples of reframing is from luxury car brand Rolls Royce. They famously decided to showcase their cars ... at yacht shows. The reasoning went thus: Rolls Royces are very high end and when people judge them at car shows in the frame of a car, against the likes of BMW, Mercedes or Audi, they appear ultra-expensive, and people therefore will judge, evaluate and decide on the basis of car-related criteria.[79]

But when set against a range of yachts, suddenly it's an altogether different context and competitive set. Compared to a yacht costing in the region of several-million dollars, a Rolls Royce suddenly looks like good value – buy one, get another for the butler.

This is the joy of reframing: take your brand out of its expected competitive arena (its positioning, if you like) and immediately different criteria are in play and different responses can be achieved.

8. VW parades its ugliness

It's nigh on impossible to talk about great advertising without summoning the presence of Bill Bernbach. We discussed his role in the development of insight in The Insight Book.

His agency, Doyle Dane Bernbach, valued wit, honesty and intelligence as the core of great advertising, rather than the didactic and rationalistic bombast that was typical of the time.

Students of advertising know of the Volkswagen campaign from 1959, which included the 'Think Small' and 'Lemon' ads. Other famous DDB campaigns included 'We Try Harder' for Avis and 'You Don't Have to Be Jewish to Love Levy's' for Levy's Rye Bread.[80]

DDB created my all-time favourite TV commercial for Volkswagen: "Snowplow," posing the question, "Have you ever wondered how the man who drives the snowplow drives to the snowplow? This one drives a Volkswagen." It remains as powerful and simple as it was when it first aired in 1964.

It's easy to choose pretty much anything from the VW back catalogue, but in this context let me just alight upon one, a full-page newspaper ad the day after the Apollo moon landing in 1969.

It featured a photo of the strange-looking lunar landing module and a VW logo, with the headline, "It's ugly, but it gets you there." No picture of the car, no glorifying blustering headline. As with Rolls Royce, but based on instinct rather than newfangled theories, Bernbach knew that was the best way of encouraging reappraisal by taking the brand out of its frame of comfort.

Not only did DDB not shy away from the ugliness of Volkswagen, they positively embraced it: "Ugly is only skin deep" was another headline in the series.

And, in the light of my obsession with personality as much as content, consider the feel of the ad: they had made the Beetle lovable in a daring, unapologetic, witty and honest way.

9. IKEA's not-so-sleepy campaign

Returning briefly to the pandemic, more and more people reported having sleep problems (unsurprisingly), prompting IKEA to produce a campaign to promote some of their sleep-related offerings, such as duvets, sheets and pillows.

In 2020, London ad agency Mother devised a series of clever and smartly designed posters featuring products such as energy drinks, anti-ageing creams and vitamin supplements – all of which are intended to imitate the effects of a good night's sleep – in outsize form but filled with Ikea bedding items replacing the liquids, pills and creams. The point being that there really are no gimmicky alternatives to the physical benefits of a good night's sleep, and that IKEA products will deliver that in spades.

Another smart demonstration of the creative opportunities afforded by reframing out of the category norms.

IT'S FUN REFRAMING

1. Reframing 45 degrees

One of the shining examples of reframing one can hope for and a story that just brings a twinkle to the heart: the case of Diamond Shreddies in Canada in 2008 and a campaign created by Ogilvy, Toronto.[81]

It starts with a classic brand conundrum for anyone ploughing the marketing furrow: Canadians didn't think Shreddies was relevant any more. The 70-year-old brand was in steady decline, and there was no product innovation to create news or interest in the brand.

But then serendipity and insight chipped in.

During one of the brainstorming meetings at the agency, Hunter Somerville, a 26-year-old intern, held up one of the Shreddies, and joked, "it isn't a square, it's a diamond."

Nancy Vonk, chief creative officer, saw something in that jokey throwaway.

And thus, Diamond Shreddies was born – a new product that maintained all the physical characteristics of the original product, but with a revamped image. The campaign for "New Diamond Shreddies" was a hit in Canada.

Now, as someone who used to work in the RTE (ready to eat) cereal market, I deeply understand the challenges of working with an old trooper like Shreddies. This is a brand that had been around in Canada for 70 years and had a fairly mundane product positioning – 100% pure wheat – and a rather worthy image to go with it. (In many countries, too, it is competing with another 100% wheat brand of some longevity, Weetabix (or Weet-Bix in Australia).

So new Diamond Shreddies was a brilliant way of shaking up this perception.

But it's flippant, fun and very uncategory-like. You may ask, "But did it work?"

The answer on so many levels is yes. It delivered 18% growth, as well as becoming a case study in textbooks and one of Canada's most recognized ad campaigns.

First, cereal is a repertoire market, it being very common for households to have a variety of them in the cupboard. So, a significant part of the marketing for a brand in this category is to serve as a reminder. This campaign was a hugely effective way of creating saliency (cutting through attention spam) for those who might be repertoire users of Shreddies but had let it drop out of their memory and off the shelf.

Second, there is *some* evidence of perceived product benefit. Shreddies created a video of a focus group discussing Diamond versus normal Shreddies and the moderator (actually an improv comedian) manages to coax out of some subjects that they expect Diamond Shreddies to taste better (semioticians will point to the inherent meaning of 'diamonds,' with their sense of luxury and wealth).

Finally, it allowed the brand to innovate creatively, something that they might have thought impossible given its long heritage and innocuous format. But as the coup de grace, they even introduced a special combo pack that mixed square and Diamond Shreddies in the same box.

Of all the ads I have discussed in training and speaking over the last few years, this is one that has the fewest nay-sayers: yes, it does tend to make us question our rationality (but then, that is one of the principal tenets of BE), but it's hard to resist its appeal.

2. The Key(s) to Reframing

Another demonstration of fun as a driver of behaviour change began with an initiative by Volkswagen in Sweden, whose goal was to show the power of fun in achieving behaviour change.[82]

But I think it has a bigger role to play in our context.

The question at the heart of this specific intervention started with a choice that many of us face on a regular basis: stairs or escalators?

Some days, it's just easier to stand still and let the escalator do the heavy human lifting for you. But what if taking the stairs could somehow be made more fun?

In 2009, advertising agency NORD DDB and car manufacturer Volkswagen noticed that the stairs at the Odenplan metro station in Stockholm, Sweden, were largely being ignored in favour of a neighbouring escalator. Hardly a rare occurrence.

They used this as a challenge to design a method to encourage commuters to use the stairs by making it fun: they would turn the stairs into a fully functional piano keyboard by installing motion-sensor piano keys. The video of people of all ages and pets messing around, being mesmerized and making music on the stairs is charming as well as illuminating.

Given this is such a universally appealing idea, it is no surprise that Piano Stairs have appeared in Auckland, Melbourne, Milan, Istanbul, Colombia and Seoul. (Why nowhere else?)

Let's unpack its success and see why it struck a chord (sorry).

- First, even as a one-off, it was a huge success. Usually, 95% of travellers took the escalator but instead 66% started choosing the stairs. There was evidence too that the behaviour lasted beyond that original occasion: once they realized taking the stairs wasn't an arduous irritation, that new behaviour became embedded.
- Contrast this with conventional behaviour-change campaigns prompting you to get more exercise. They are usually big, hectoring and chastizing campaigns on TV or billboards, suggesting a variety of health benefits and/or warning you of the health risks if you don't keep fit. Or maybe throwing in a sustainability angle (it's less ecologically wasteful taking the stairs). All very System 2, all containing some element of finger-pointy criticism.
- There is none of that tone of voice here. In fact, it is defined by an absence of 'content,' messaging or factual transmission of any sort. Nothing that makes you feel inept. Instead, it is all about playfulness, satisfaction and reward: you learn to carry out the desired behaviour and, in the process, find pleasure and joy.

- Note too that the behaviour change comes first. The attitude change – oh, it seems that I don't hate exercise – follows the adoption of the new behaviour.

Another of Volkswagen's Fun Theory experiments was building the world's deepest rubbish bin. Whenever rubbish was dropped into it, it triggered a sound-effect in that it made a cartoon-like falling-off-a-cliff noise, before emitting a 'dung' sound when it finally and dramatically reached the bottom. This was intended to make it (more) fun to throw away your rubbish.[83]

It was a huge success, so much so that members of the public actually started collecting discarded litter to drop in the bin, just for the fun of it.

As the video explains, some 72 kilos of rubbish was put in the bin during one day, which was 41 kilos more than the closest standard trash bin. People were actively going out of their way to carry out the behaviour that was previously considered undesirable.

Making recycling fun is, superficially at least, more about the fun of the action than the dangers of plastic pollution in our oceans. What matters is the end result, the action, not why that action was taken. If someone recycles a plastic bottle because it is fun or feels good, the bottle is no less recycled than if they acted through fear for the planet. When that feel-good action becomes a spontaneous habit – job done.

OKINAWA MELODY ROAD

Lastly, one of my key favourite examples of rewarding good behaviour is the so-called Melody Roads in Japan.[84] There are now in the region of 30 of these musical roads, spread throughout Japan, from Hokkaido to Okinawa. Devised by a team from the Hokkaido Industrial Research Institute after a serendipitous discovery by an engineer who accidentally dug furrows in a highway, they are stretches of road that produce music from a system of grooves dug in the road and the vibrations produced as vehicles drive over them.

As well as road signs alerting motorists to the incoming musical tune, all the Melody Roads have musical notes painted on the surface of the road. There are a few other musical roads around the world, from California to South Korea, but Japan has the widest range.

This clever musical nudge works in various ways: as a way of curbing speeding (over a certain limit the music doesn't play), as well as helping to keep drivers awake while driving.

Which explains ...

- *Why we can see the same things in a completely different light if they are framed differently: high-end car or millionaire's luxury? Migrant or refugee? Ninety-five per cent fat free or 5% fat? Pro-life or pro-choice? Is Amex a credit card or a social badge (or both)?*

So instead, we need to ...

- *Think carefully if we want our brand, service or policy to be reconsidered, to take it out of its usual frame to disrupt how people comfortably see the brand, service or issue. Can you have a premium adult ice cream? Make people see condoms as a financial investment?*
- *And never discount the possibility that fun and playfulness are powerful levers of reframing.*

YOU CAN'T HANDLE
THE TRUTH!

PART THREE

CONCLUSIONS

The irony that many marketers are susceptible to their own form of confirmation bias regarding these theories – why change what we've done for decades? – is not lost on me.

I am used to the sound of apple carts not being overturned from distrust of novelty.

As I like to say, with a hint of the Marvel Cinematic Universe: change is strange.

But what might a theory of behaviour change look like that we can all – clients and agencies, communicators and senders – subscribe to?

NEW CHALLENGES TO THE OLD ORDER

There are some undeniable challenges posed by adopting these theories and principles, and we have to be honest enough to face and accept them.

ACKNOWLEDGING THE ILLUSION OF CONTROL

Perhaps the biggest challenge philosophically to how we carry out the business of influence is to our sense of control. The assumption has been that as consumers (and obviously beyond), we are in control of our thoughts, intentions and actions and therefore our job is to merely shift people's behaviour by appealing to their sense of control. But if the unconscious System 1 is the 'secret author of our choices,' that becomes far trickier and ethically complex to boot.

This is even without mentioning memes, an almost incidental coinage by Richard Dawkins to postulate cultural transmission as analogous to genetic transmission, as part of a 'universal principle of self-replicating entities.'

Though perhaps not the originator himself (some credit Nicholas Humphreys with the idea), it has swept from a philosophical postulate to a global unit of currency of cultural transmission or imitation. (I always had a soft spot for big thinker and 'strange loop'-er Douglas Hofstadter breaking it down to "Me! Me!".) The viral model of behaviour is certainly catching, even if you have never experienced Rick Astley.

The meme, even if it is hard to pin down, is another attack on the sovereignty of self as it is based on the idea that what survives and succeeds is the most powerful idea, not necessarily what is most true (we will come to 'truth' soon). Hence, it further punctures the illusion that we are in control of our ideas, and for those of us involved in behaviour change, we are not in 'control' of those we seek to influence.

THE (BRAIN'S) WAR ON TRUTH

"The brain gravitates towards solutions that are designed to match not only data but desire."

Drew Westen[85]

Troubling and inconvenient as it may feel, truth does not emerge with much of its authority intact. Without entering the debate about the post-truth world, or what US talk show host Stephen Colbert named 'truthiness' – the belief in what you feel to be true rather than what the facts will support (see also *The Inspiratorium*[86]), examined from a brain-centred viewpoint, truth looks less important than we like to think. As Robert Wright said, the brain prefers victory to truth. Objective truth and reality are only part of the apparatus the brain applies for making decisions and navigating the world. Hence, our old friends confirmation bias and cognitive dissonance once again loom large: it is not that truth doesn't count or matter, but simply that the brain may be predisposed to stick with what it believes to both save energy (it takes a lot to change our minds), and to preserve our sense of rightness.

The implications are many and profound. Not the least of them is the need to redress how we see truth and facts in the process of behaviour change. Just giving people more facts, repeating them or expecting the sheer accumulation of them to be effective – for example, show how bad smoking is for you – is not going to work in this new world. We can see this flaw apparent in so much communication, not just in the behaviour-change domain, relying as it does on merely shipping units of information.

Accepting the limitations of facts and truth means activating feeling and delving into the rich currents of meaning, which is more creative and malleable than truth. One can also add into the mix the old journalistic adage, "Just because it's true doesn't make it interesting."

One final thought that is part of my Golden Thread across all my books and thinking: the idea that we allocate way too much time to *content* (what we say) and not nearly enough to *form* (how we say it). In this context, that means accepting that messaging of facts is only part of any communication, and that form and frame are as core to effecting behaviour change.

RECONSIDER RATIONALITY, RETHINK RESEARCH, REWARD REPUTATION

TOWARDS A
NEW MODEL

So, what might a new model or theory of consumer behaviour look like?

At the risk of preaching for a GUT or TOE, we can at least prepare something in accordance with EO Wilson's *Consilience*[87] – a convergence of different domains and disciplines.

Let's identify six foundations for understanding consumer behaviour.

1. HUMANS ARE NOT COMPUTERS BUT COMPLEX ADAPTIVE SYSTEMS.

- I have talked elsewhere about the default belief that the human brain is a computer and how pernicious that metaphor is. We are not processing machines that work sequentially, independently and logically.
- Nobel-laureate, physicist and Santa Fe complexity guru Murray Gell-Mann – the man who coined the word 'quark' after a passage in James Joyce – talks of people as being 'Complex Adaptive Systems' (CAS).
- In this way, he believes, there are universal similarities among some of the most crucial processes on Earth: biological evolution, ecological systems, the mammalian

immune system, the evolution of human societies and sophisticated computer software systems to name but a few. What links all of these processes is that each relies on gathering information about itself and its interactions with its environment, building as it goes a model or schema of the world around it based on regularities it perceives. So, in the case of human individuals, we think, learn, use symbolic language and generate new generations of CAS in our wake (chief among which are powerful computers and their descendants, such as AI). Later on, he adapts the term to include CAS that act as an interpreter and observer of the information; this he calls an IGUS, an Information Gathering and Utilizing System.

- Another metaphor might be that the brain is a Reputation Management Mechanism, acting as our legal defence team.

2. WE NEED TO RETHINK RATIONALITY.

- We need to rid ourselves, our businesses and our communications of the lingering but pernicious admiration for Homo Economicus. As wryly expressed by Nobel Prize winning Economist Daniel McFadden, the image of the ideal who is "sovereign in tastes, steely-eyed and point-on in perception of risk, and relentless in maximization of happiness" must be allowed to be put out to pasture, never to interfere with our understanding of human behaviour again. Better to go with Geoffrey Miller's more caustic summary: "We are insecure, praise-starved flattery sluts."[88]

- However easy and natural it feels, resist the temptation to think that the role of communications is to bombard people with facts and tell everyone everything everywhere all at once (one for film fans). This is based on the spurious precepts of Homo Economicus and can lead to the belief that *If they only had more/the right facts* ... This can often be expressed in that slippery word 'education', which appears in so many strategies and creative briefs. The challenge is to 'educate the consumer'. No, it isn't: that implies being didactic and admonishing.
- Perhaps the most pragmatic approach is to follow the words of Jonathan Swift we cited above. He claims that humans are *'animal ... rationis capax'*: merely *capable* of reasoning.
- So, by implication, rationality is not something we necessarily exercise on a regular basis. To paraphrase Charles Darwin, we may be called creatures of reason, but more appropriately, we would better be seen as creatures of habit.[89]

3. REPUTATION OVER RATIONALITY.

- If rationality is not the royal road to change, what is?
- Well, one candidate is the appeal not to reason but to reputation. This is sometimes known as impression management, whereby we/the brain takes it upon itself to create the best possible impression of ourselves by influencing the perception of others; and in so doing will go to great-to-any lengths to make people like us. So much of what we do is performed in the pursuit of not truth or virtue but to bolster and boost reputation.

- Borrowing Dean Burnett's expression, our brains make us want to be liked, to be superior and to be consistent.[90] Other factors are purely secondary.

- Having explored Geoffrey Miller's cheeky neologism 'Status-ticians' elsewhere, I will just cite it again (re-cite)? But let us never forget, in our race to look rational and respectable, that much of what we do is to enhance our status in order to display our social and sexual fitness for evolutionary goals.

- Let's maybe revive an approach first devised by eclectic scholar James G. March and outlined in his *A Primer on Decision Making*.[91] Essentially it is an identity model of behaviour change. Here the identity – who and what you identify with – supersedes the 'consequences model,' which relies on messages you receive about what is best for you. The issue at hand here is: Who am I? What kind of situation is this? What would someone like me do in this situation? So, the role of communication is not a series of persuasive instructions but helping people answer how they can make the change a matter of identity and not consequences.

- As Jonathan Haidt[92] puts it, there are two ways of getting to the truth: the way of the scientist and the way of the lawyer. Lawyers start with a conclusion they want to convince others of and then seek evidence that supports it. In this view, the brain is a pretty good scientist but is an outstanding lawyer.

- My own epigrammatic summary of this approach is: massaging beats messaging.

4. REWARD REWARD.

- Always aspire to a rewarding tone of voice.
- One clue that your communications will falter is if it feels any of the following: instructional, didactic, pedagogic, patronizing or judgmental. Too much communication feels very much parent-to-child, and any parents reading will know how well *that* works.
- Think very carefully as the tonal component of your behaviour-change campaign is crucial and often fatally misunderstood. The reasons Piano Stairs and other successful approaches cut through attention spam and initiate behaviour change is that they accentuate positive emotions and rewards, rather than activating negative feelings of resistance and dismay.
- As Nina Simone would confirm, feeling good is key to behaviour change. We revel in what makes us feel good, so a good choice makes us feel good about that choice but also makes the brain feel reassured – via cognitive ease – and therefore reinforces wellbeing. Example: when I worked on advertising for the Peugeot car marque, we knew that any communications to launch a new model had (at least) three goals: to encourage purchase of the new model, to make people feel good about choosing that model, but also to reassure and reinforce the positive feelings and choices of anyone who already owns any Peugeot.

5. RETHINK RESEARCH.

- Is it any surprise that so much market research is lacking insight, unsurprising and unactionable? I like to use the term 'un-sight' for this condition. (See *The Insight Book*.)

- At the very least, we have to acknowledge that if our marketing and communications activity depends on the results of market research, and that market research depends on only speaking to System 2, then we had better gird ourselves for results that are at least partial, and at worst wholly misleading. We are unreliable witnesses – it's not just that we willingly lie when asked to explain our behaviour or intentions, it's more that – entombed as they are in System 1 – we very often simply don't have access to them and can only confabulate a story that may or may not have some relationship to the truth.

- The research industry – or at least its more enlightened outposts – have acknowledged this issue and are exploring approaches that tap into System 1. So do try and seek enlightenment from these avant-garde thinkers; if not, just tear up your research budget or spend it on Taylor Swift re-releases.

6. NEVER IGNORE CONTEXT.

- Any decision-making must take into account the importance of context. We are so obsessed with content that we sometime forget the importance of 'where.' People who often mistakenly simplify Behavioural Economics as 'just psychology' fail to appreciate the fact that many decisions are not triggered *inside* the brain but *outside* it.

- Any research approach that rests on assumptions that context does not affect decisions will also be sadly disappointed. We know that so many of our decisions are triggered not by what goes inside our head, but what happens outside. Whether we are with friends, family, at a football match, in a work situation, different contexts will produce different decisions, no matter.

- This is sometime known as the micro-macro problem, often considered to be a central problem of sociology and underappreciated by classical economics. Namely, that the model that economists rely on focuses on a single 'representative' actor, which ignores the complexity of interactions between agents (aka people).

- And so much of the economy, so much of the dance of our decision-making happens at the intersection of the individual and the social. We need look no further than how everything from fashions, to ideas, to political positions diffuse through a process of cascades (often labelled 'emotional contagion').

TOWARDS AN INTEGRATIVE THEORY

So, to better understand and therefore influence consumer behaviour, what might follow the death knells of Homo Economicus and the sacred worship of efficiency? We are not yet to replace it definitively, but at least acknowledging its shortcomings (in marketing, research, sales, persuasion) has to be a good starting point.

We need, I suggest, an integrative theory that includes:

1. **Identity theory.** As we have outlined throughout the book, persuasion must go beyond the logical, rational and didactic. Identity theory – for all the critiques it has received in the political arena – has a role to play.

2. **Semiotics.** Understanding the role that signs, symbols and meanings play in perception and (therefore) behaviour.

3. **Anthropology.** A science that looks at groups sharing tribal meanings, symbols and totems and (in our case) how we can better understand both brands and people's behaviour towards and with them.

4. **Complexity sciences.** To rid our business of the obsession with linearity, transportation models of behaviour (like AIDA) and simple cause-and-effect assumptions. Complexity and chaos theories provide a reminder that small inputs can have disproportionately large (and unpredictable) outputs.

- This also reminds us of the importance of feedback and complexity theory. One of the most exciting developments in the scientific arena is the science of complexity and emergence. All this followed, in terms of complexity theory, in the emergence of global patterns from simple rules.

- It is worth noting that one of the central tenets of complexity and systems thinking is that small world networks may lack an organizational centre, yet global interactions still take place. What this means is that old, cherished notions of hierarchical control at the individual level do not necessarily apply. One implication in the corporate area is the assumption inbred into generations of 'scientific managers' that their role is based on *controlling* their organizations, their brands and their 'consumers' needs to be revised. Its talk of leverage strikes a chord with those in this industry who see that like does not always generate like; sometimes small movements can have massive effects (and vice versa).

- And while we are looking to attack linearity, let's recall the central thesis of John Kay's book *Obliquity*[93]: that often our ends can be best achieved if we address them indirectly and obliquely, rather than aiming directly for behaviour change, happiness or success.

- And surprise and chance can also be part of our persuasion armoury. Too often the dead of logic should be paused, and serendipity and surprise be introduced to shake up and disturb habits and create novelty, which can cut through attention spam.

5. **Evolutionary psychology.** Much of what we referred to earlier comes under the aegis of 'evo-psycho', the principle that much of our behaviour is primed (unconsciously) by instincts, drives and emotions that are serving the interest of evolution as much as (often more than) what feels to be our own personal needs.

6. **Art.** Maybe not quite at the same level, but if we are serious about the challenge of understanding and changing behaviour, let's not exclude the possibility that more art can be as beneficial as more science.

AND FINALLY

In his book, *Darwin's Dangerous Idea*,[94] the philosopher Daniel Dennett makes a good case that Darwinism (specifically the modern synthesis of Neo-Darwinism) is indeed the "single best idea anyone has ever had." He memorably described it as a 'universal acid' that affects everything it comes into contact with.

I believe that, especially in a time when the alluring promises of Big Data have led some to pronounce 'The End of Theory,' we need some broadly accepted understanding and theory of human behaviour and decision-making that we can all agree on before we launch into internal comms, external comms or any form of activity that aims to change behaviour.

I hope to have shown that Behavioural Economics promises to be *that* universal acid and *that* theory.

ENDNOTES

1. Stephen Jay Gould, *Bully for Brontosaurus* (1991)

2. Chris Anderson, article:
   https://www.wired.com/2008/06/pb-theory/

3. Anthony Tasgal, *The Insight Book* (2023)

4. Barbara Ehrenreich, *Smile or Die* (2009)

5. Oscar Wilde, *The Decay of Lying* (1891)

6. JBS Haldane, *The Journal of Genetics* (1963) The 4 Stages of Acceptance

7. David Eagleman, *Incognito* (2011)

8. Anthony Tasgal, *The Storytelling Workbook* (2022)

9. David Sloan Wilson, interview: https://evonomics.com/scientists-discover-what-economists-never-found-humans/

10. Paul Samuelson, *Newsweek* (1966):
    https://quoteinvestigator.com/2023/11/01/predict-nine/#:~:text=The%20old%20joke%20that%20'Macroeconomists,in%20%E2%80%9CNewsweek%E2%80%9D%20in%201966.

11. Arnold Bennett, Journals, entry for 18 March (1897)

12. Cass Sunstein and Richard Thaler, *Nudge* (2008)

13. Dan Kopf, article:
    https://qz.com/1418336/its-been-10-years-since-behavioral-economics-hit-the-mainstream

14. Donald Marron, article:
    https://www.forbes.com/sites/beltway/2015/09/16/
    obama-nudge-government/

15. Aditya Chakrabortty, article:
    https://www.theguardian.com/politics/2008/jul/12/economy.
    conservatives

16. MINDSPACE: UK Cabinet Office, 2008

17. Thomas Carlyle, 1849 essay

18. Lisa Feldman Barrett, *How Emotions Are Made* (2017)

19. Antonio Damasio, *Descartes' Error* (1994)

20. Timothy Wilson, *Strangers to Ourselves* (2002)

21. Antonio Damasio, *Descartes' Error* (1994) and *The Feeling of What
    Happens* (1999)

22. Friedrich Hayek, *The Fatal Conceit* (1988)

23. Cordelia Fine, *A Mind of Its Own* (2005)

24. Tiffany Watt Smith, *The Book of Human Emotions*, (2015)

25. David Hume, *Treatise of Human Nature* (1739)

26. TH Huxley (attrib)

27. Adam Phillips, *Promises, Promises* (2002)

28. Hugo Mercier and Dan Sperber, *The Enigma of Reason* (2017)

29. The Socratic elenchus:
    https://www.thoughtco.com/elenchus-argumentation-1690637

30. Wason test:
    https://www.socialpsychology.org/teach/wasona.htm

31. Sir William Hamilton, 1865 (cited in Timothy Wilson,
    Strangers to Ourselves, 2002)

32. Time Headline:
    https://time.com/3937351/consciousness-unconsciousness-brain/

33. Daniel Kahneman, *Thinking, Fast and Slow* (2011)

34. Keith Stanovich, Richard West: 'Individual Differences in Reasoning: Implications for the Rationality Debate?' (2000)

35. Jonathan Haidt, *The Happiness Hypothesis* (2006)

36. Chip and Dan Heath, *Switch* (2010)

37. Brian Wansink, "Bottomless Bowls: Why Visual Cues of Portion Size May influence intake" (2005)

38. Control your eating: https://www.newscientist.com/article/mg22530030-700-forget-the-fads-the-easy-way-to-control-your-eating/#.VLQu9ifik7B

39. Robert Epstein: https://www.theguardian.com/uk/2003/feb/16/ameliahill.theobserver

40. Epstein: cited in Richard Wiseman, *Rip It Up* (2012)

41. Dutton, D. G., & Aron, A. P. (1974). "Some Evidence for Heightened Sexual Attraction Under Conditions of High Anxiety." *Journal of Personality and Social Psychology*, 30(4), 510–517. https://doi.org/10.1037/h0037031

42. Oliver Sacks, *The Man Who Mistook his Wife for a Hat* (1985)

43. Pink Floyd, "Brain Damage" from Dark Side of The Moon, originally released 1973

44. Timothy Wilson, op.cit

45. Bat and Ball experiment Shane Frederick: https://www.theguardian.com/science/2020/oct/19/can-you-solve-it-the-bat-the-ball-and-the-bamboozle and https://www.aeaweb.org/articles?id=10.1257/089533005775196732

46. Daniel Kahneman, op.cit.

47. Daniel Wegner, *The Illusion of Conscious Will*, (2002)

48. Wegner, "How to Think, Say or Do Precisely the Worst Thing for Any Occasion," *Science*, July 2009

49. Wilmore funeral home ad:
https://edition.cnn.com/2021/09/21/us/covid-vaccine-billboard-funeral-home-ad-agency-trnd/index.html

50. Catalogue of 92 definitions of emotions:
https://link.springer.com/article/10.1007/BF00992553

51. Lisa Feldman Barrett, op.cit

52. Cordelia Fine, op. cit.

53. British Heart Foundation ads:
https://www.bhf.org.uk/what-we-do/our-research/research-successes/smoking-and-heart-health and https://www.campaignlive.co.uk/article/british-heart-foundation-shows-fatty-truth-abouts-crisps/594113

54. Elizabeth Loftus memory experiment:
https://theaksk.medium.com/the-car-crash-experiment-38b01e499930#:~:text=The%201974%20Car%20Crash%20Experiment,were%20eyewitnesses%20to%20the%20scene.

55. Memory experiments: Wade, K.A.; Garry, M.; Read, J.D.; Lindsay, D.S. (2002). "A Picture is Worth a Thousand Lies: Using False Photographs to Create False Childhood Memories."

56. Memory experiments: "When Photographs Create False Memories," Maryanne Garry and Matthew P. Gerrie, Victoria University of Wellington, Wellington, New Zealand

57. Daniel Gilbert:
http://www.newscientist.com/article/mg21929310.400-i-could-have-sworn-why-you-cant-trust-your-memory.html#.UhjCXnbm3U1

58. Rabbie Burns: "To A Louse, On Seeing One on a Lady's Bonnet at Church" (1786)

59. Hot Cold empathy gap: George Loewenstein, "Hot Cold Empathy Gaps and Medical Decision Making," *Health Psychology,* 2005

60. Eric Hoffer, *The Passionate State of Mind* (1955)

61. Conformity experiment:
https://www.simplypsychology.org/asch-conformity.html

62. Groucho Marx "who you gonna believe?":
https://quoteinvestigator.com/2018/07/31/believe-eyes/#:~:text=Dear%20Quote%20Investigator%3A%20According%20to,been%20attributed%20to%20Groucho%20Marx.

63. More on conformity:
https://www.simplypsychology.org/asch-conformity.html

64. "Ditto" Xmas display:
https://www.thesun.co.uk/news/17032337/christmas-tree-funny-decoration/ and https://www.popularmechanics.com/home/outdoor-projects/a30274028/neighbor-ditto-christmas-lights/

65. Candid Camera elevator stunt:
https://www.openculture.com/2016/11/the-power-of-conformity-1962-episode-of-candid-camera-reveals-the-psychology-of-riding-elevators.html

66. Dan Ariely, *Predictably Irrational* (2008)

67. Alcohol Education Project:
http://www.alcoholeducationproject.org/posters/posterschools.htm

68. Opower energy saving:
https://inudgeyou.com/en/green-nudge-the-classic-social-comparison-experiment-by-opower/ and https://slate.com/technology/2013/03/opower-using-smiley-faces-and-peer-pressure-to-save-the-planet.html

69. Robert Cialdini, *Influence: The Psychology of Persuasion* (1984)

70. UK government use of social norms for COVID campaign:
https://www.gov.uk/government/news/new-tv-advert-urges-public-to-stay-at-home-to-protect-the-nhs-and-save-lives

71. General framing papers: Tversky A, Kahneman D. "The Framing of Decisions and the Psychology of Choice." *Science*, 1981; Levin IP, Gaeth GJ. "How Consumers are Affected by the Framing of Attribute Information Before and After Consuming the Product." *J Consumer Research*, 1988.

72. Medical framing: *Redelmeier, D. A. Rozin, P. & Kahneman, D.* (1993). "Understanding Patients' Decisions: Cognitive and Emotional Perspectives." *Journal of the American Medical Association*, 270, 72–76

73. Stephanos Bibas, *Harvard Law Review* :
    https://www.jstor.org/stable/4093404

74. Soda sizes:
    https://slate.com/technology/2012/06/bloomberg-bans-large-sized-
    soda-the-science-behind-the-decision.html

75. Carmen Piernas and Barry Popkin, "Food Portion Patterns and Trends
    Among U.S. Children and the Relationship to Total Eating Occasion Size,"
    1977–2006

76. Airline profits vs burger:
    https://twitter.com/colinalewis/status/1198267551765188608/photo/1

77. Toronto burger:
    https://www.snopes.com/fact-check/toronto-burgers-office-supplies/

78. Trojan vs nappies ad https://imgur.com/gallery/F7VfTkC

79. Rolls Royce cars at Yacht shows:
    https://theislander.online/2016/07/c83-news/
    prestige-cars-displayed-on-the-car-deck-at-the-monaco-yacht-show/

80. VW Beetle lunar module:
    https://www.hemmings.com/stories/
    volkswagen-beetle-lunar-lander-advertisement/

81. Diamond Shreddies:
    https://www.ivanpols.com/case-shreddies and
    https://creativehalloffame.org/works/diamond-shreddies/

82. Piano stairs:
    https://nudges.wordpress.com/2009/10/09/musical-stairs/ and
    https://www.designoftheworld.com/piano-stairs/

83. Deepest bin:
    https://www.valens-research.com/dynamic-marketing-communique/
    the-worlds-deepest-bin-find-out-how-this-campaign-encouraged-a-fun-
    cleaning-activity-in-2009-thursdays-gorillas-of-guerrilla-marketing/

84. Melody Road:
https://www.theguardian.com/world/2007/nov/13/
japan.gadgets and https://detour-roadtrips.com/home/
rattle-and-hum-five-musical-roads-that-play-as-you-go

85. Drew Westen, *The Political Brain* (2007)

86. Anthony Tasgal, The Inspiratorium (2018)

87. EO Wilson, Consilience (1998)

88. Geoffrey Miller, Spent: Sex, Evolution, and Consumer Behavior (2009)

89. Charles Darwin, *Letters* (1856)

90. Dean Burnett and Chip Heath, *Happy Brain* (2018) and *The Idiot Brain* (2016)

91. James G. March: *A Primer on Decision-Making* (1994)

92. Haidt, J. (2001). "The Emotional Dog and Its Rational Tail: A Social Intuitionist Approach to Moral Judgment." Psychological Review, 108(4), 814 -834. https://doi.org/10.1037/0033-295X.108.4.814

93. John Kay, Obliquity (2010)

94. Daniel Dennett, *Darwin's Dangerous Idea* (1995)

ACKNOWLEDGEMENTS

Thanks as ever to Martin for stalwart support over nearly a decade (yes) and tolerating all the etymological asides, and to Clare and Aiyana for suffering through the edits with unexpected calmness and grace.

To Nikki, Josh, Zach and Saskia for getting used to what must feel like an iteratively tiresome process.

And in memory of Will, our cat, who brought us so much joy.

ABOUT THE AUTHOR

Anthony "Tas" Tasgal is a man of many lanyards: trainer, author, TEDx speaker, brand/comms strategist and lecturer.

He is a course director for the Chartered Institute of Marketing, the Market Research Society, the Institute of Internal Communication, the Civil Service College and the Chartered Institute of Procurement and Supply.

He is a global speaker, having done his first TEDx talk in Newcastle in November 2023, and regularly reviews the papers and contributes on marketing and communications subjects on TalkTV.

He specializes in storytelling, Behavioural Economics, insightment and, as a lapsed Classicist, he also indulges in etymology and Homer (not the yellow one).

He also runs *The Guardian* masterclass on "Harnessing the power of storytelling" and is a brand ambassador for Home Grown Club in London.

He works for clients as varied as the BBC, Nokia, Panasonic, The Royal Albert Hall, EE, Visit Scotland, Boehringer Ingelheim, Yamaha, Sky, Veolia, The Intellectual Property Office (UK Govt), ReLondon, the NHS, Mouser Electronics, ABB (industrial automation), Destination New South Wales and Westpac (Australia).

He is the author of the award-winning *The Storytelling Book*, which has sold over 35,000 copies globally, *The Inspiratorium*, *InCitations*, *The Storytelling Workbook* and, in 2023, *The Insight Book*.

The Customer Behaviour Book is his sixth book.

He speaks passable French and some Italian, plays tennis, skis harmlessly and has recently indulged in performing stand-up comedy.

Tas can be found loitering at **@taswellhill** and **https://www.linkedin.com/in/tastasgal/** and you can read about him here on *The Guardian* website, **bit.ly/GuardianMeetTas.**

BY THE SAME AUTHOR

ISBN: 978-1-911498-46-9

ISBN: 978-1-912555-57-4

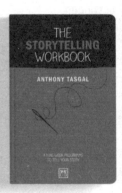

ISBN: 978-1-912555-97-0

ISBN: 978-1-911687-97-9

ISBN: 978-1-911687-38-2